Psychodynamic Approaches in Health and Social Care

Psychodynamic Approaches in Health and Social Care sees experienced psychoanalysts, psychotherapists and educationalists analyse classic psychoanalytic papers and accessibly apply them to contemporary health and social care settings.

In each chapter, practitioners and educators analyse a classic paper to support a better understanding of and resolution to the complex, pervasive and multi-faceted challenges facing contemporary health and social care provision. The papers include works from some of psychoanalysis' most important thinkers.

The novel approach in this book will make for an illuminating read for those working in health and social care settings with limited prior knowledge of psychoanalytic and psychodynamic approaches and for practising analysts and therapists looking to apply their knowledge in contemporary health and social care.

Shelly Allen is a senior lecturer in mental health nursing and psychological therapies at the University of Manchester, UK and a psychodynamic psychotherapist in independent practice.

'What a wonderful and creative idea for a book! *Psychodynamic Approaches in Health and Social Care* offers readers an exploratory yet highly relevant and practical approach to working through and thinking about key psychoanalytic concepts in health and social care practice. It does this through a process of thinking with key texts that offer readers a range of fertile and provocative insights when working in mental health care. Providing case vignettes and relevant examples from practice, the book provides a compelling and timely assertion of the relevance and centrality of psychoanalytic concepts for everyday practice. Too often in recent years, psychodynamic approaches have been consigned to an unread repository of supposedly antiquated knowledge, but this book reawakens an interest in a vital tradition and returns readers to the source texts with a renewed vigour and relevance. I hope it will be read and discussed widely in all areas of mental health scholarship and practice.'

Alastair Morgan, *Senior Lecturer in Mental Health at the University of Manchester UK, author of* Continental Philosophy of Psychiatry: The Lure of Madness *(Palgrave Macmillan, 2022).*

'This book calls for an honest dialogue between individual care workers and their teams so as to improve the quality of their work. The failures of past educators and managers who dwelt solely on the performative aspects of health and social care, whilst disregarding its emotional and relational components, are now obvious. Drawing on the classic works of psychodynamic theorists, each chapter presents the essence of their thinking and how their ideas can be assimilated into practice. This engaging book has the power to revolutionise caring environments and merits a place on multiple reading lists and in all relevant workplaces. I highly commend it.'

Dr Peter Nolan, *Professor of Mental Health Nursing (Emeritus), The University of Staffordshire. York, 2025*

'This book will be invaluable to mental health nurses and allied practitioners, illuminating a deeper understanding of the relational dynamics of everyday practice. A psychoanalytic perspective is the most sustained and tested body of knowledge that informs a trauma informed approach to practice.'

Professor Gary Winship, *Education, Trauma & Mental Health, School of Education, University of Nottingham, Editor-in-Chief,* British Journal of Psychotherapy

'This book is an essential, accessible guide for health and social care professionals, at all levels, introducing key psychoanalytic knowledge and practice insights. Through gathering classic papers and skilfully bringing concepts to life with illustrative case examples, the editor reveals how useful and applicable psychoanalytic concepts are in helping make sense of contemporary practice dilemmas and realities. I strongly recommend this straightforward and enjoyable book for practitioners and students across any practice disciplines who are keen to explore what psychoanalytic theory and practice has to offer.'

Dr Helen Hingley-Jones, *Associate Professor, Middlesex University*

'The professions and occupations within social work, nursing, and health and social care have been beset by the comings and goings of a range of different theoretical perspectives in the last fifty years; some helpful, some less so. Ideas informing practice derived from psychoanalysis have bubbled along under the surface, occasionally coming up for air. So, what a pleasure to have this new contribution addressing the usefulness of such ideas to inform practice, with the hope of improving the circumstances of those in receipt of services and interventions, and those providing them.'

Dr Helen Cosis Brown, *Fostering and Adoption Panel Chair and Fostering Service Decision Maker, previously Professor of Social Work at the University of Bedfordshire*

Psychodynamic Approaches in Health and Social Care

Applying Classic Psychoanalytic Work to
Contemporary Settings

Edited by Shelly Allen

Routledge
Taylor & Francis Group

LONDON AND NEW YORK

Designed cover image: Wood Carving by John Sharples, Photograph by Shelly Allen

First published 2026
by Routledge
4 Park Square, Milton Park, Abingdon, Oxon OX14 4RN

and by Routledge
605 Third Avenue, New York, NY 10158

Routledge is an imprint of the Taylor & Francis Group, an informa business

British Library Cataloguing-in-Publication Data
A catalogue record for this book is available from the British Library

ISBN: 978-1-032-89198-9 (hbk)
ISBN: 978-1-032-87952-9 (pbk)
ISBN: 978-1-003-54166-0 (ebk)

DOI: 10.4324/9781003541660

Typeset in Times New Roman
by Apex CoVantage, LLC

In memory of mum and dad and for family.

Contents

Contributors

Shelly Allen

Position and affiliation: Senior Lecturer in Mental Health Nursing and Psychological Therapies at the University of Manchester and Psychodynamic Psychotherapist

ORCID iD: https://orcid.org/0000-0002-3140-170X

Dr Shelly Allen is a Senior Lecturer in Mental Health Nursing and Psychological Therapies at the University of Manchester and a psychodynamic psychotherapist in independent practice. Shelly uses psychodynamic psychotherapy to support health and social care practice and education, coupled with an interest in psychodynamic and systemic approaches to organisations.

Pat Cartney

Position and affiliation: Head of Social Work, University of Manchester

ORCID iD: https://orcid.org/0000-0002-0564-1881

Dr Pat Cartney is Head of Social Work at the University of Manchester with strategic responsibility for the delivery of all pre- and post-qualifying social work programmes. She has a keen interest in teaching psychodynamic thinking and exploring how students might use these ideas to enrich their social work practice.

Alasdair Forrest

Position and affiliation: Consultant Forensic Psychiatrist and Medical Psychotherapist, Royal Cornhill Hospital, Aberdeen

ORCID iD: https://orcid.org/0000-0003-4615-6310 [orcid.org]

Dr Alasdair Forrest is a group analyst. He is a consultant forensic psychiatrist and medical psychotherapist to the Royal Cornhill Hospital, Aberdeen, and visiting psychiatrist to HMP & YOI Grampian.

Celeste Foster

Position and affiliation: Associate Professor/Reader in Mental Health Nursing

ORCID iD: https://orcid.org/0000-0002-5005-5419

Dr Celeste Foster is Associate Professor for Mental Health Nursing at the University of Salford. A mental health nurse, psychodynamic therapist and researcher working in child and adolescent mental health since 1995. Published outputs take psychoanalytic approaches to working with adolescents, relationally focused care, self-harm and developmental trauma.

Martin Gill

Position and affiliation: Fellow IOPA. BPC Registered Psychoanalyst. Director of Training Bpf North. Associate Lecturer, Tavistock & Portman NHS Trust. Clinical Lead Six Degrees Social Enterprise

Martin Gill is a Psychoanalyst working in private practice in Manchester. Martin is also a supervisor, lecturer and teacher holding roles in psychodynamic and psychoanalytic training programmes across the UK.

Suryia Nayak

Position and affiliation: Dr Suryia Nayak: Senior Lecturer Social Work and Group Analyst

ORCID iD: https://orcid.org/0000-0002-5940-1322

Dr Suryia Nayak, Senior Lecturer in Social Work, Psychoanalytic Psychotherapist, Clinical Supervisor, group analyst and feminist activist, has over 40 years' experience of applying the Black feminist intersectionality.

Naomi Sharples

Position and affiliation: Associate Dean, School of Health and Society, University of Salford

Professor Naomi Sharples leads the academic and international developments for the School of Health and Society at the University of Salford. Passionate about inclusive education and global health developments, Naomi is a recognised leader in her field of global health education.

Acknowledgements

This book is a collaborative piece of work; it relied on the generosity of all contributors in taking time to consider and present aspects of their work in such a thoughtful and thought-provoking way, for which I am very grateful.

The book is based on our work and experiences with people who use services, students and colleagues; these stories form the fabric of the book. Thank you to all who supported the inclusion of their experiences in the case examples and participants in the psychoanalytically informed reading group, who allowed us to use our reflections from talking and thinking together.

Finally thank you to Zoe Meyer and Routledge Taylor & Francis Group for being so encouraging in supporting the idea for the book and its completion.

Shelly Allen

Introduction

Shelly Allen

This book is aimed at those working in health and social care who are not necessarily familiar with psychodynamic approaches derived from psychoanalytic theory. The chapters are written from the perspectives of those who have experience of teaching psychodynamic approaches across diverse student populations, and who are familiar with considering their own practice using these ideas and/or work clinically as therapists.

In thinking about psychodynamic approaches, this definition offers a context in terms of its therapeutic use:

> Psychodynamic psychotherapy is distinguished from other models in that it focuses primarily on unconscious aspects of our behaviour that lead to internal conflict, as well as how we experience, regulate and express our emotions in an interpersonal context, including in the therapeutic relationship.
>
> (Abrahams & Rohleder, 2021, p. 2)

This book takes these fundamental tenets of psychodynamic practice and applies them to contemporary health and social care. In doing so, it aims to bring psychodynamic approaches to life through the application of classic papers to situations which will be familiar to those who work in health and social care. Each chapter takes a specific paper on which to base consideration and application to a case example before drawing more widely on the theoretical underpinning to tease relevant issues out further.

The chosen papers have been extensively cited in other works; we have used these papers in our teaching, reading groups and clinical practice. The papers are accessible without a specialist library membership, and this was important to us in trying to bring these key concepts to an audience who are not usually immersed in psychodynamic approaches. This is not to exclude those who are familiar with psychodynamic psychotherapy; we think there are gains to be had for this audience too.

Taking an applied focus, much as we do in our teaching of psychodynamic concepts, each chapter begins with a contextual 'everyday' focus in the form of a composite case example, which protects confidentiality whilst also reflecting an authentic issue within health and social care. The intention is to promote interest

DOI: 10.4324/9781003541660-1

and engagement through familiarity before moving on to the theoretical underpinning. We hope that this will help contextualise ideas and bring them to life. The case examples we have used take a diverse and broad approach to reflect some of the challenges in contemporary health and social care: some relate to individuals who use services; others take an aspect of practice where the impact is felt by practitioners. We consider leadership, teams, groups and an organisational context, and we reflect on our experiences of using psychodynamic approaches in education to support practitioners and provoke thought and discussion through reading groups.

We believe this book is well timed given the challenges facing contemporary health and social care provision, which are complex, pervasive and multi-faceted. Internationally, these challenges have undoubtedly been impacted by the global pandemic and are subject to fiscal complexities which drive expressed priorities and decision making for populations across the globe.

Using the United Kingdom (UK) to illustrate this point further, the situation has been compounded by a programme of austerity and the impact of Brexit, which has consequently made attracting and recruiting those committed to a career in health and social care onto educational programmes and the subsequent retention of experienced staff, hugely problematic.

The corollary of this has been felt in the inequity of access to health and social care, and lengthy waits for treatment throughout the population. This inequity leading to increased morbidity of physical and mental health issues, increased mortality, and with these pressures, we have witnessed a lack of opportunity for practitioners' access to support and development, all of which makes for a challenging, disturbing, and at times, hostile environment in which to work.

This experience for staff in health and social care is expressed through vacancies and widespread strike action in relation to pay, conditions and the ability to deliver the primary task, this being the provision of high-quality, personalised, integrated health and social care which is both effective and acceptable to those in receipt of it. It is a situation which the National Health Service Confederation (2022) referred to as a system on the cliff edge and, according to the Care Quality Commission (2022), one that is gridlocked to the point of clearly causing a negative impact on how people experience care within the sector.

In this ever-changing, uncertain, complex health and social care landscape there are seldom any givens. However, it can be stated with confidence that health and social care relies on people. It is for this reason that psychodynamic approaches in their applied state, as derived from psychoanalytic theory, have the potential to be an invaluable source of support in enabling those who work in health and social care to meet the primary task.

Psychoanalysis, developed by Sigmund Freud in the late 19th century has undergone a wealth of theoretical and clinical development since that time, by Freud, those who worked beside him and beyond. Its utility is characterised by these developments and represented in psychodynamic approaches as a clinical treatment for people experiencing a wide range of mental and physical distress individually, as a couple, and in groups, both familial and other. It has also been shown to assist in enabling an understanding of social defences, leadership, teamwork and organisational behaviour and culture.

It is safe to say that psychoanalysis can evoke strong opinions both in support for and in the denouncement of. Such criticism is not new; it has lived alongside the development of psychoanalytic theory since its conception and has been fiercely debated within the clinical arena. In 2012, *BMJ* posed the question of whether psychoanalysis had value in modern mental health services. Peter Fonagy and Alessandra Lemma were called upon to be the proponents for, and Paul Salkovskis and Lewis Wolpert provided the counter-argument.

Fonagy and Lemma (2012) argued that psychoanalytic concepts can support staff in providing high-quality services despite the interpersonal pressures to which they are exposed. Such concepts can help with responding in humane ways when experiencing stress and anxiety and assist in understanding why things go wrong in therapeutic relationships (Fonagy & Lemma, 2012). This fits with the purpose of this book in that we want to share how psychodynamic approaches, derived from psychoanalytic theory, are a source of support where the impact of the work is emotionally challenging.

In terms of the counter-argument, Salkovskis and Wolpert's (2012) proposal was largely based on clinical rigour, and it is reasonable to suggest that in just over a decade since the *BMJ* posed this debate, progress has been made in answering this critique. The British Psychoanalytic Council (BPC, n.d.) provides a range of evidence to support psychoanalytic and psychodynamic therapies including a helpful summary which states that psychodynamic and psychoanalytic treatments continue to benefit long after therapy is completed. It has been found that other models of therapy may be effective because psychoanalytic techniques and processes are used to support their delivery. Longer-term psychoanalytic psychotherapy, for one year or more, is more effective than shorter forms for the treatment of complex mental disorders. Further, psychoanalytic psychotherapy has promising findings in relation to supporting people with a diagnosis of personality disorder. Finally, mentalisation-based therapy, which is a form of psychoanalytic psychotherapy, has positive results for those diagnosed with personality problems (BPC, n.d.).

Psychodynamic concepts lend themselves to a thoughtful, supportive engagement with the challenges facing contemporary health and social care provision described above. This was reiterated more recently by Peter Fonagy:

> In my view, psychoanalytic theory that underpins psychodynamic psychotherapy is the richest and most sophisticated set of concepts concerning the functioning of the human mind that we currently have available to us.
>
> (in Abrahams & Rohleder, 2021, p. xiv)

Psychodynamic concepts within health and social care are applied not only in interactions between individuals but also in understanding the dynamics which influence individuals, groups and organisations in everyday work settings. It is this utility that makes psychodynamic concepts so compelling within the contemporary context of care. This is endorsed by The Tavistock Institute of Human Relations (n.d.) stating:

> How humans relate to each other and non-human systems, how we grow in character, how we embrace learning and change, are questions which flicker around all points of world history.

As such, the application of psychodynamic concepts proposed is not about becoming a "pseudo-psychoanalyst" but about applying theory to assist in understanding, particularly when it feels non-sensical and troubling. Psychodynamic concepts provide a language for expressing individuals' experiences, bewilderment and needs. They offer a framework through which to describe and enquire about those of another and the ability to share a hypothesis and which makes understanding possible. This may be informally with peers and through more formal concepts such as reflective work discussion groups. This provides the opportunity for others to offer perspectives point out blind spots or ask probing questions to deepen understanding.

In short, the application of psychodynamic concepts is about engendering and supporting a healthy curiosity about oneself, others and the organisations where work takes place. In turn, this can lead to a questioning attitude which supports those who work in health and social care to remain mindful of the complex dynamics which they are both subject to and contribute to.

It is for these reasons discussed that a text which takes key psychoanalytic concepts derived from classic papers and applies them to the challenging context of health and social care can provide a framework for enabling connection. Such connection can be enabled intrapersonally; interpersonally and in relation to groups, teams and organisations. Taking this approach, a text which is accessible and written in an applied way in its form and content has the potential to help those working in health and social care to make sense of the challenging bewilderment and disturbance that can be evoked by the nature and context of the work.

Taking an intersectional approach which reflects society will ensure that the book is applied in a way that is sensitive to the experiences of its members. Belkin (2020, p. 7) poses the question 'Who are you', which I urge you to keep at the forefront of your mind as you read this book, relating its contents to your experiences and those you work with and support in whatever context that takes place. The intention is to encourage a space for considering similarities and differences with acknowledgement that these are dynamic, not owned by one or the other but fluid in our relationships with each other and the structures of society. This is not to deny experiences of discrimination, prejudice and privilege but to encourage a reflective stance that acknowledges that we all play a part in its complexity.

Inviting the reader to consider its application within their own context supports connection and offers an argument against the critique that psychoanalytic theory, from which psychodynamic approaches derive, is elitist and outdated.

This book is organised in chapters based on one classic psychoanalytic paper which is then applied to contemporary health and social care. The selected papers are presented chronologically to reflect the development of psychoanalytic and in turn psychodynamic concepts across the decades. The title of each chapter references the paper around which discussion is organised. This enables readers to identify areas that are particularly pertinent to them should this be the preferred way to engage with the book.

Abrahams and Rohleder (2021) state that Freud revolutionised the treatment of mental health and developed a metapsychology of human development and behaviour. The use of classic papers in this book means that psychoanalytic theory is drawn upon throughout. However, as introduced earlier, psychodynamic approaches derive from Freud's original theory and just like Abrahams and Rohleder, who distinguish between psychoanalytic and psychodynamic, we choose to use the term psychodynamic. This reflects an approach which draws on psychoanalytic theory and is applied beyond the analyst–analysand relationship.

There is a long history of applying psychoanalysis beyond its use as a clinical intervention. Isabel Menzies Lyth's study on social defences for mitigating anxiety in a general hospital in the 1950s is just one classic example. Since this seminal study, a wealth of evidence has demonstrated this theory (Sher & Lawlor, 2022). In short, the use of psychodynamic concepts to understand everyday issues has history, utility and applicability across a wide-ranging contemporary context.

The journey to the point where classic psychoanalytic papers that have had a personal influence in our clinical work and application within education has been accompanied with the experience of how sustaining it is to draw on psychoanalytic approaches in everyday work. It is this that we are keen to share at a time when globally, health and social care is under enormous pressure, and for me, this started some time ago.

As a qualified mental health nurse and university lecturer, I had been interested in psychodynamic ways of understanding long before I completed my clinical training. I found myself drawn to these ideas in my PhD and later attended a course focused on psychodynamic approaches to working with adolescents. This was formative in cementing the usefulness of psychodynamic concepts in understanding my everyday work beyond clinical situations.

I used what I was learning on the course in my work with students; it helped me understand, make meaning, and be attentive to boundaries when the line between lecturer and nurse felt somewhat blurred. At this point, it seems reasonable to offer the experience rather than talking around it. What follows are excerpts from a paper submitted to the course to show how I was using psychodynamic approaches to my work; aspects have been amended to protect confidentiality. It is hoped that doing this will orient the reader to the format of chapters to come.

Case example

Josie is an 18-year-old first-year undergraduate at the university where I am employed as a lecturer and her personal tutor. Josie requested to discuss a personal issue with me that she was struggling with. It transpired that a few days earlier, she had elected to terminate a pregnancy. Josie and I are not engaged in a clinical relationship we are in a lecturer-student dynamic.

Pines (1988) remarks that despite advances in contraception, a significant number of teenage girls become pregnant. Many experience psychic growth due to the normal developmental crises of puberty and adolescence followed by pregnancy and motherhood. For others, such crises revive primitive anxieties which, compounded by the demands of pregnancy and motherhood, lead to pathological solutions and difficulties in mothering and motherliness rather than healthy developmental growth (Pines, 1988).

As Josie's personal tutor, an appreciation of this dynamic helped me to make sense of her presentation and have a more thoughtful response to her, thereby striving to both gain and give understanding (Joseph, 1983).

Conflicting experiences of separation, individuation and identification are commonplace in adolescence, but for a pregnant teenager, this perplexing experience can be even more difficult. Emotional readiness for parenthood comes later in life than the physiological possibility of giving birth, which follows puberty (Hurley, 2010). This was reiterated to me when I met Josie during university fresher's week and was subject to tales typical of this transition into undergraduate life. I warmed to her and had a sense of her excitement and anticipation of this exciting new life away from home. I readily connected with memories of my university experience and needed to be attentive to my countertransference, my thoughts, feelings, behaviour and responses evoked by connection with Josie.

Issues of separation, competition and identification lead to consideration of the Oedipal complex, which may re-emerge in adolescence (Briggs, 2002) and require reworking (Copley, 1993) if development is to be attained (Lemma-Wright, 1997). Josie's reference to her mother was in the context of not sharing her difficult experience, and, interestingly, her father was not mentioned at all. Josie told me that she had shared her experience with a sibling and an aunty, but her anxiety was not contained. Copley (1993) describes Bion's theory as the ability to contain the infant's fear and anxiety by attending to the baby using a thoughtful and emotional response; this is referred to as *reverie* and does not solely relate to infancy but also adolescence (Briggs, 2002).

However, Josie did not experience this: she said her aunty 'did everything wrong'.

I had to monitor my response during the conversation with Josie due to my countertransference and the pull I felt to respond. I felt irritation with the aunty whom I had never met and vulnerability to what I understood to be a projection from Josie. I also considered my own experiences of trying to support friends who were unable to gain the support of parental figures, leaving me to feel a weight of responsibility to 'get it right' for them.

I understood my experience of having felt what Josie found unbearable through its projection and communication to me as she rid herself of the associated pain of feeling let down by her aunty and feeling shameful. This powerful unconscious process could have prompted a response from me; however, I have become increasingly attentive to countertransference and projective identification. I was able to monitor myself and thereby resist a pull to disparage the efforts Josie's aunty made. This was particularly important because it could have damaged our future relationship if Josie perceived me to have attacked her aunty.

Freud (1917) proposed similarities between mourning and melancholia with one exception: the disturbance of self-regard, which is absent in mourning. The sense of shame and regret conveyed to me by Josie included the observation that the nurses at the hospital were judgmental of her. This relates to Freud's critical agency, later to become the superego. This disturbance of self-regard is a clear indication of how she felt about the situation and herself (Freud, 1917). In considering Freud's classic paper, it may be reasonable to suggest that Josie cannot mourn her loss whilst at the same time experiencing melancholia due to the circumstances in which this loss has occurred. This perversion in the capacity to mourn (Lemma & Levy, 2004) risks identification with the lost person in an abusive way (Freud, 1917). The consequences of this are that Pines's (1990) contentions regarding depression, hatred and loss of self-esteem may be brought to fruition, particularly if Josie is not helped to resolve this traumatic experience.

As Josie's personal tutor, my role is not explicitly the resolution of her difficulties, but there are strategies that I have used in support of it. I have been able to bear Josie's distress, the containment of which is crucial in relation to trauma (Garland, 2004). I have monitored my own response (Pines, 1990) to ensure it is supportive and useful rather than engaging in a damaging enactment (Joseph, 1983), and I have expanded my knowledge through completion of this work in an effort to gain and give understanding (Joseph, 1983). The opportunity to speak of the experience has been provided, and in doing so, the telling of the story may help to begin the journey to face loss, grief and rage (Stubley, 2004).

My understanding of Josie's experiences, which are replete with loss and trauma that permeate adolescence – including pregnancy and the termination – has deepened through completion of this work, which can only help in my capacity as Josie's personal tutor.

In presenting this case example as part of the introduction to the book, the intention was to show how psychodynamic approaches can be used in the everyday work of health and social care beyond its clinical application. It is this which drove the idea and momentum of the book, and I hope that the reader will connect their own experiences with the points discussed here and in the chapters that follow.

We bring ten classic psychoanalytic papers to the audience as a way of sharing key concepts in an applied and contemporary way. The implications and recommendations at the end of each chapter are intended to support practice and assist in identifying and managing the everyday challenges evoked by contemporary health and social care. If whilst reading the book, there is a sense of familiarity and interest as a result, then the aim of bringing these ideas to a contemporary audience will have been achieved. The challenge which follows is then to process this experience and use it to help secure support in sustaining oneself to provide high-quality health and social care. This is in keeping with Freud's (1914) contention, which is the paper we start with in Chapter 1, that insight is not enough: something needs working through for its full impact to be felt.

References

Abrahams, D., & Rohleder, P. (2021) *A Clinical Guide to Psychodynamic Psychotherapy.* London & New York: Routledge; Taylor & Francis Group.

Belkin, M. (2020) Who is queer around here? Overcoming rigid thinking and relating in patient and analyst. In Belkin, M., & White, C. (eds) *Intersectionality and Relational Psychoanalysis.* London & New York: Routledge; Taylor & Francis Group.

BPC (n.d.) https://www.bpc.org.uk/information-support/the-evidence-base/. Accessed 29th April 2025.

Briggs, S. (2002) *Working with Adolescents: A Contemporary Psychodynamic Approach.* London: Palgrave Macmillan.

Care Quality Commission. (2022) https://www.cqc.org.uk/sites/default/files/2022-10/20221024_stateofcare2122_print.pdf. Accessed 29th April 2025.

Copley, B. (1993) Adolescence a process of change. In *The World of Adolescence. Literature, Society and Psychoanalytic Psychotherapy.* London: Free Association Books.

Fonagy, P., & Lemma, A. (2012) Does psychoanalysis have a valuable place in modern mental health services? Yes. *BMJ*;344:e1211.

Freud, S. (1914) Remembering, repeating and working through (further recommendations on the technique of psycho-analysis II). *The Standard Edition of the Complete Psychological Works of Sigmund Freud*;12:145–156.

Freud, S. (1917) Mourning and melancholia. In *The Standard Edition of the Complete Psychological Works of Sigmund Freud, Volume XIV (1914–1916): On the History of the Psycho-Analytic Movement, Papers on Metapsychology and Other Works*, 237–258. Hogarth Press & The Institute of Psychoanalysis.

Garland, C. (2004) Traumatic events and their impact on symbolic functioning. In Levy, S., & Lemma, A. (eds) *The Perversion of Loss Psychoanalytic Perspectives on Trauma.* London & Philadelphia: Whurr Publishers.

Hurley, A. (2010) Reparation by Proxy: Experiences of working with pregnant teenagers and adolescent mothers. *Journal of Child Psychotherapy*;36(2):101–118.

Joseph, B. (1983) On understanding and not understanding: Some technical issues. *International Journal of Psycho-Analysis*;64.

Lemma, A., & Levy, S. (2004) *The Perversion of Loss Psychoanalytic Perspectives on Trauma.* London & Philadelphia: Whurr Publishers.

Lemma-Wright, A. (1997) *Invitation to Psychodynamic Psychology.* London: Whurr Publishers.

National Health Service (NHS) Confederation. (2022) https://www.nhsconfed.org/publications/system-cliff-edge-addressing-challenges-social-care-capacity accessed 29th April 2025.

Pines, D. (1988) Adolescent pregnancy and motherhood: A psychoanalytic perspective. *Psychoanalytic Inquiry*;8(2):234–251.

Pines, D. (1990) Pregnancy, miscarriage and abortion: A psychoanalytic perspective. *International Journal of Psycho-Analysis*;71.

Salkovskis & Wolpert's. (2012) Does psychoanalysis have a valuable place in modern mental health services? No. *BMJ*;344:e1188.

Sher, M., & Lawlor, D. (2022) *An Introduction to Systems Psychodynamics Consultancy Research and Training.* London & New York: Routledge Taylor & Francis Group.

Stubley, J. (2004) Bearing the unbearable: Melancholia following severe trauma. In Levy, S., & Lemma, A. (eds) *The Perversion of Loss Psychoanalytic Perspectives on Trauma.* London & Philadelphia: Whurr Publishers.

Tavistock Institute of Human Relations (n.d.) https://www.tavinstitute.org/. Accessed 29th April 2025.

Chapter 1

'Remembering, Repeating and Working Through' (Freud, 1914)

Promoting curiosity and remaining engaged

Shelly Allen and Martin Gill

Introduction

In this chapter, we show how 'Remembering, Repeating and Working Through' (Freud, 1914), one of the papers Freud wrote on technique, can offer a framework for promoting curiosity and understanding in contemporary health and social care. We see this as a way to remain engaged with the issues presented when working with people who access services, particularly when this troubles those tasked with providing care.

These troubles manifest in a number of ways such as concern about what might happen to the service user, family members, and those around them in the form of risk. There may be a lack of connection with those providing care because the issues are outside of the practitioner's experience and/or skill set. This may lead the practitioner to respond in ways that do not support the primary task of providing high-quality, personalised care to those who need it.

It is not unreasonable to suggest that this may manifest as frustration, particularly in overwhelmed services when best efforts seem to reap little benefit. The person and family have had all the service perceives can be offered, yet still the difficulties persist, leaving workers feeling disheartened. We propose that this is not an unusual experience, and that due to the impact on workers, and therefore people who use health and social services, it warrants consideration in helping to make sense of what is happening in these moments.

As stated in the introduction to this book, psychodynamic approaches can be used to gain an understanding of the emotional impact on practitioners when working in health and social care. We think that Freud's (1914) 'Remembering, Repeating and Working Through' is particularly helpful in gaining an appreciation of the dynamic that compels people to repeat mistakes and continue to engage in unhealthy relationships and behaviours despite the best efforts of practitioners trying to support them, and it is to this classic paper that we turn our attention.

Freud (1914) is concerned, at least in part, with technique, but many who read this chapter will not be trained in psychodynamic approaches. Rather than this being a hindrance, we propose that the essence of this paper, that the person repeats what cannot be remembered through action, is relevant to all who support people in health and social care. Whilst we are not proposing a simple cause-and-effect relationship, we do know that people who use health and social care services have

DOI: 10.4324/9781003541660-2

often had difficult early experiences. Psychodynamic approaches take an interest in these early experiences and their relevance to the service user's current presentation. This is where Freud helps by offering a way to think about these early experiences and how they are impacting the person's life in the here and now. This is where Freud's insight into remembering and repeating is relevant.

The other main theme of the paper is that change will not come from insight alone, that this recognition needs to be worked through. Freud (1914) articulates this in the words of battle, historically relevant given the timing of this paper with the start of World War I, when he writes 'one cannot overcome an enemy who is absent or not within range' (p. 152). The aim of remembering what has been forgotten – understanding its repetition, how it shows itself through action and consequently to work through it – is the domain of psychoanalysis and psychodynamic psychotherapy. It can take lengthy periods of therapy to gain this deep level of understanding, and the intention here is not to diminish this.

Clearly, merely engaging with this paper does not mean that technique can be acquired: it is not about becoming a pseudo-psychotherapist. Rather, we propose that it is as important to know one's limitations as it is to recognise the resources available to support service users. We are proposing that 'Remembering, Repeating and Working Through' can help engender and support a healthy curiosity about oneself, others and the organisations in which the context of work takes place. In doing, it can provide a framework for understanding what underlies and drives what the person is presenting through their action.

In relation to this, we propose that gaining familiarity with the concepts in 'Remembering, Repeating and Working Through' enables a framework and language for wondering about others' experiences and sharing a hypothesis about what might be happening that contributes to making understanding possible. This is particularly important when the practitioner's understanding is that the service user seems unable to accept the help offered and effect change in their lives. The technique at the heart of 'Remembering' relies on sharing what could be considered stories, which has the potential to deepen insights into the dynamics of work (Cardona, 2020).

Our sharing of stories, which supports the points being made in this chapter, was through a psychoanalytically informed reading group and which we will detail in the following case example.

Case example

We jointly facilitate a reading group. The flyer invitation asked potential participants if they had an interest in the application of psychoanalytic theory in health and social care. We advertised this in a university School of Health Sciences and Business School, where we knew there was an interest in the subject area. We also invited participants from a social enterprise who provide psychological interventions to support mental health care.

The format is monthly with five pre-selected papers which participants are informed of at the beginning. The premise is clear: participants do not need to be experienced in the theory; the only requirement is to read the paper beforehand and bring ideas evoked through its reading for discussion in the group, which lasts one and a half hours.

We have consistently had between five and eight participants excluding ourselves. Participants have been psychological practitioners, psychotherapists, undergraduate and postgraduate students and university staff. It has been a diverse group with rich discussion, and we have been confident that there is an appetite for sharing stories and ideas prompted by classic psychoanalytic papers in the application of contemporary health and social care. 'Remembering, Repeating and Working Through' was the first paper we read and discussed together.

What follows are our reflections on the group's discussion, the themes which emerged and how we have come to understand what resonated with participants. We have changed some details to protect confidentiality. We are not trying to present a verbatim account of the group discussion. Rather, we are sharing our memory of it and the impression we were left with. By reflecting this in what follows, we hope to support our proposal that 'Remembering' has much to offer in contemporary health and social care.

Freud's (1914) 'Remembering, Repeating and Working Through' was introduced whilst considering that the group consisted of diverse professional backgrounds, and whilst there was an interest in psychoanalytic theory, they were not trained within this modality. The paper was introduced by drawing attention to Freud's argument that remembering does not necessarily follow from actual cognitive memory but can emerge with action or doing, what psychodynamic clinicians might describe as enactment; an example will follow shortly. Freud covers several important psychoanalytic concepts including the compulsion to repeat, which is in turn linked to the transference and resistance.

As part of introducing the paper, we attempted to bring into view the relevance of Freud and psychoanalytic concepts in a contemporary situation. Freud draws attention to how remembering alone is not enough to bring about psychic change, contending that working through is crucial. Despite being neglected at times, it is an essential element within clinical practice and the interventions delivered.

This was initially taken up within the group in terms of interventions that take a cognitive behavioural therapy (CBT) approach. On reflection, this being the first group, setting, tone and familiarity were being established, and given that a number of group members worked in services delivering CBT interventions in the UK National Health Service (NHS), this was not surprising. This is further reinforced when considering the availability of different types of therapy within health and social care with a predominance of CBT approaches within the NHS.

This was the most frequently delivered therapy in England during 2022–23, accounting for 41.3% of all courses of therapy in the year. Compared with modalities which take a psychoanalytic orientation such as interpersonal psychotherapy (1.1%) and brief psychodynamic therapy (0.27%) (digital.nhs.uk, 2022–23), it is clear to see why this perspective was initially taken up by the group: it reflected the wider, dominant contemporary clinical orientation within the NHS.

We oriented the group to the idea of considering remembering more widely as part of a complex psychic system, which implicitly includes recognition of the unconscious, and this was taken up thoughtfully by the group. We illustrate this shortly in relation to the vignette and impressions shared by participants.

The concept of resistance as a defensive strategy which unconsciously keeps painful experiences out of mind was linked to a consideration of neuroses, which can loosely be thought of as distress associated with anxiety and depression, and the psychodynamic understanding of the unconscious. Having provided a foundation to the concepts which are integral to Freud's (1914) paper, the group then turned to a discussion of how contemporary mental health services are configured. This focused on the way that episodes of care were understood in a fragmented way rather than the whole being greater than the sum of its parts.

That is, a person may have multiple referrals to services for bouts of depression over a number of years; within the current model, each episode is considered separately, and each treatment episode and intervention is also seen through this reductive lens. By opening the discussion using 'Remembering', group participants began to consider this aspect more fully and moved to consider a wider developmental lens, the links here with 'Remembering, Repeating and Working Through' and early childhood not being lost on us. As a group, we were then able to advance ideas concerning possible resistance to treatment, with participants sharing their curiosity as to why previous interventions had not been successful even though they had been delivered using established treatment protocols.

By supporting the group in thinking differently using transference, the direction of feelings, desires and phantasies from formative relationships such as with parents onto the practitioner, we were able to refer to the points made by Freud as follows:

> We soon perceive that the transference is itself only a piece of repetition, and that the repetition is a transference of the forgotten past not only on to the doctor but also on to all the other aspects of the current situation.
>
> (Freud, 1914, p. 151)

Linking this to countertransference – the feelings and emotions stirred up in the practitioner in relation to the service user (King, 1978), resistance and necessary defences against pain and overwhelm, and locating these within the ordinary clinical situation – the group was able to begin to consider a different perspective on several themes, including why the patient does not get better even though the intervention has been delivered correctly and the countertransference effect of this on the clinician, and in turn linking the impact of feeling clinically ineffective and hopeless in the clinical situation to burn out and stress. This enabled a deeper and wider consideration of the complexity of psychic change that was not solely levelled at the practitioner's efficacy or otherwise.

Following this, one participant brought forward a clinical example related to a secure setting where a female service user would routinely remove her clothing prior to contact with a male member of staff, appearing naked in what was felt as a disturbing, shocking and ultimately shaming experience for all involved. This was a visceral example which the group quickly began to discuss drawing on themes from 'Remembering, Repeating and Working Through'. Briefly commenting on the woman's history to maintain confidentiality, she had a history of sexual abuse and had acquired several diagnoses related to the diagnostic classification of personality disorder.

The discussion focused on the emotional response of the staff member, which was understood by the group participants as countertransference through the lens of a parallel process within the group. Feelings of anger, shame and humiliation came into view. It was then possible to develop a hypothesis within this to elaborate how the service user was using a number of actions which could be understood through psychodynamic concepts including projection and repetition compulsion. This was contrasted with more mature defences such as sublimation, an example being channelling aggression into a sport such as rugby and the use of humour by making light of a painful experience (Abrahams & Rohleder, 2021).

By appearing naked, the service user shocked and disturbed the staff member, who then felt angry and rejecting and underneath this, ashamed and humiliated; the staff member consequently complained bitterly about having to deal with this person. The staff member felt used, possibly abused, by what was understood as a concerted and planned attack on them. They were described as feeling flooded with negative, hot feelings leading to a desire to disengage and reject the female service user.

With time and space away from the immediacy of this hot situation, we were able to consider it more fully as a group by triangulating the known aspect of the woman's history of sexual abuse, with the action in the present. Considering the experience from a psychodynamic perspective enabled a hypothesis to form which linked with a repetition of earlier shame, humiliation and objectification. With further testing of this hypothesis, the group could see how it might potentially contribute to a psychodynamic formulation and shared a sense that this could lead to a better understanding of the crucial elements being acted out. The provocative nakedness, alongside the shared emotional responses of shame, humiliation and hatred in both the woman and the male member of staff who was forced to take a part in this visually provocative demonstration of a memory.

The group felt and discussed how finding a different perspective through drawing on the concepts in 'Remembering, Repeating and Working Through' enabled a more thoughtful and emotionally engaged stance from which it was possible to find a more empathic position in relation to both parties in the dynamic. Participants could see how this enhanced understanding of what was happening might reduce the heat of the situation and anger, help to better consider who was being shamed by whom, and what the function of the re-enactment was concerned with.

Having considered 'Remembering, Repeating and Working Through' (Freud, 1914) through the experience of the reading group and illustrating the application of key concepts which we feel confident will be familiar to those who work in health and social care. We will now place this in the wider context of the paper to provide a further foundation on which to base our discussion which follows.

Overview of the paper

Freud's (1914) paper begins with a précis of psychoanalytic developments to date, most of which remain central as contemporary treatments that provide an environment, bound by a therapeutic frame where free association is welcome, thereby guarding against the analyst or therapist dictating the content, pace or rhythm of what happens during that time. As such, the focus relies on what is on the patient's mind. The therapist/analyst uses skilled listening to recognise the resistance, this being the mechanism to keep out of conscious awareness what has been repressed; it is a process of shutting out of painful thoughts, feelings and memories, threatening or shameful experiences that cannot consciously be borne by the person. Using interpretation, the therapist/analyst offers a view on what is at the heart of the troubles experienced by the patient in relation to themself and others. By working with resistance, there is an opportunity to allow what was shut out into conscious awareness with a possibility that with support, it may eventually be overcome and bearable.

Freud (1914) then details different types of forgotten 'memories', and as in the paper, this chapter focuses on those that are not reproduced as a memory but instead are acted out repeatedly without conscious awareness that it is happening. We propose, just as illustrated in the reading group, that this is a pattern frequently encountered in health and social care which troubles practitioners. It is said that this paper was the first appearance of a crucial concept: 'compulsion to repeat' (Freud, 1914, p. 150). Examples of this include a persistent pattern of harmful relationships, violence directed towards others, self-destructive patterns of varying severity, essentially the things that people do to prompt others to wonder, why do they keep doing that?

Freud goes on to develop this point further by stressing that the way to curtail the compulsion to repeat and allow whatever has been repressed to be remembered is through the transference, the unconscious attribution of feelings and emotions from formative relationships such as parents onto the therapist or any caregiver: 'We render the compulsion harmless, and indeed useful, by giving it the right to assert itself in a definite field. We admit it into the transference' (Freud, 1914, p. 154).

It is here, in what Freud terms this intermediate region, that the transition between illness and real life can take place. Whilst we are not advocating working with transference in the absence of clinical training to do so, we have shown how the concepts included in 'Remembering' can open up perspectives to something that might otherwise feel troubling and hopeless, and it is this that we now advance through the following discussion in an effort to promote curiosity and engagement even with highly disturbing aspects of presentation.

Discussion

In the following discussion, we propose that a psychodynamic perspective can enable a more thoughtful response to what can be frustrated attempts to assist those who access health and social care services.

Guarding against enactments and repeating patterns

As detailed in the case example, where the actions of those using services trouble and provoke an impactful response in the worker, this must be managed. When under pressure, we are all subject to employing defence mechanisms, the unconscious strategies such as denial that we all use to protect ourselves from anxiety, fear, shame and overwhelm. This can be highly seductive; after all, under usual circumstances, who would choose psychic pain and suffering when it could be avoided? Yet we know that these strategies, whilst preferred, also have negative consequences associated with the avoidance of the reality of a situation.

When defensive manoeuvres predominate in health and social care services, conflicts, ineffective communication and distraction prevail. This undermines the primary task, coupled with poor leadership, sickness and absence and increased likelihood of mistakes, all of which impact care (Ballatt, Campling & Maloney, 2020).

Returning to the case example of the woman in secure care, she used her body to communicate rather than words, which requires conscious engagement with the issue of concern to describe what we identified as shame and humiliation through the intrusive experiences she had endured and over which she had no control. This is linked to Freud's contention that the ego, which we can understand as the mostly conscious, rational self that mitigates between instinctual unconscious impulses and the desire for gratification driven by the id, with our conscience and moral code is first and foremost a bodily ego (Freud, 1923). What Freud meant by this is that our early experiences are felt bodily before we can consciously link them with the words we use to describe our thoughts, feelings and emotions. Developmentally, this is how a baby experiences its needs for food, warmth, comfort, all crucial for survival. In an everyday example, we may feel self-conscious and awkward; it may be difficult to put this into words, but we can feel it as we blush – we have little control over the hot flush that happens when embarrassed.

An understanding of the use of the body to portray internal states gives the presentation of the woman in the case example a different perspective. It becomes communicative rather than solely about provocation, particularly if we draw on the defence mechanism of projection, which enables an unbearable state to be conveyed to another thereby ridding the person of the associated pain. As an example, when the person who feels inferior at work accuses a colleague of doing a poor job, the colleague then becomes the problem; all attention is diverted from the accuser elsewhere, and the accuser gets to rid themselves of the discomfort associated with lacking expertise.

Relating this back to the case example, we can hypothesise that the shame, humiliation and lack of control experienced by the woman with a history of sexual abuse was projected into the worker, with his response being a crucial part of this mechanism. An extension of this is where the projected state is identified with and the worker himself complains of being humiliated, having no control over this intrusive experience. This being an example of projective identification, this final stage ridding the woman from this painful and disturbing experience.

Whilst we understood this in the reading group as an undoubtedly disturbing experience for the male worker, he was able to put this into words and share it with colleagues and those tasked with offering support. This is a far healthier way to try to manage such an experience for the worker and service user than claiming to be unaffected or worse, perpetuating the cycle of abuse. Working with 'patients', to be understood as any service user who is in contact with health and social care, can get under the 'skin of staff' (Dartington, 2017, p. 169). Defensive manoeuvres to manage this risk becoming dysfunctional: they get in the way of doing a good job and contribute to abusive relationships and relatedness to vulnerable others. It is here that concepts from psychoanalytic theory are helpful when working in systems of care (Dartington, 2017).

Working through with a psychodynamic perspective

Freud (1914) makes it very clear that just knowing about something is only part of the picture; for change to follow, the issue needs working through.

From a psychodynamic perspective, working through can be understood as an iterative process where the same ground is covered many times. For example, breaks in treatment are likely to create disturbances especially for people with complex difficulties. Understanding and managing the complex emotional responses around breaks and transitions is a central part of the treatment process, and it is here that a psychodynamic perspective can offer insight. There is of course a bias in this book that we are advocating a psychodynamic approach: of course we would say that. However, it is not just our position: 'In my view, psychoanalytic theory that underpins psychodynamic psychotherapy is the richest and most sophisticated set of ideas concerning the functioning of the human mind that we currently have available to us' (Fonagy, in Abrahams & Rohleder, 2021, p. xiv).
Again, one might say that as a professor and psychoanalyst, Peter Fonagy would say this. Therefore, at this point we turn to the available evidence base; this indicates that approaches such as psychodynamic and psychoanalytic therapies reap benefits. There is a considerable improvement long after treatment is completed known as the sleeper effect. Non-psychoanalytic forms of therapy may be effective because psychoanalytic techniques and processes are used in the delivery. Longer-term psychoanalytic psychotherapy for one year or more is more effective than shorter forms of therapy for the treatment of complex mental disorders; psychoanalytic psychotherapy has promising findings in relation to supporting people with personality disorder. Finally, we draw attention to mentalisation-based therapy as a form of psychoanalytic psychotherapy, and which has positive results for those diagnosed with personality problems (BPC).

It is clear, however, that psychodynamic psychotherapy is not as widely available as it is relevant to the issues that bring people into contact with health and social care; as such, whilst there can been seen to be a legitimate demand, availability curtails impact. That aside, possessing the knowledge and framework to help workers to remain curious and engaged with the issues presented by service users draws on Peter Fonagy's thoughts just discussed. If we can promote ideas that can help understand the complexities and difficulties facing health and social care workers, then there is a start of a thoughtful conversation, and when that happens, there is the possibility of demonstrating a desire to understand. As a service user in receipt of this, the experience may be quite different from one where the ability to understand is curtailed by concerns of being disturbed, which may then lead the practitioner to rejection and the service user to disengagement.

It is also possible that understanding the need to work through prevents workers from feeling helpless; it is not that they are not doing a good job but rather that the help required is of a specific kind. As a caveat though, this needs to be thoughtful and engaged rather than a defence against poor-quality care.

Power of the group

The power of the group relates to its impact on how people experience health and social care and in meaning making when we come together to support a shared understanding, such as that in the reading group.

The impact of troubling experiences on those working in health and social care has the potential to be nurturing and supportive as well as damaging and abusive. Taking an intersectional approach urges consideration of the woman in the clinical example and the whole, complex interplay of all experiences that she embodies. When her provocative behaviour becomes separated from her own traumatic history, there is a risk that she becomes vilified, subject to retaliation, possibly re-traumatised and maybe abused further. This links to Ballatt, Campling and Maloney's (2020) contention that the effect of the group is often underestimated, and with a poor understanding of this impact, it is crucial to consider how kindness can be facilitated or undermined by the group dynamic.

The experience of the reading group when considering the clinical example was one where the disturbance of the enactment could be held in mind whilst also understanding it in the context of trauma. This meant we could think about it together, reflective spaces being key to enabling this stance.

Implications and recommendations

Space to work it through

The importance of a reflective space for digesting the disturbing experiences of working with those who access health and social care cannot be denied. There are several forms this can take, and one that we focus on here is work discussion. This is facilitated taking a psychodynamic approach and is common in the preparation to become a psychodynamic psychotherapist. That said, facilitating this with students who are not undergoing psychodynamic training confirms it has utility across a broad spectrum of experiences.

The use of psychoanalytic work discussion groups has a rich history where the facilitator helps the group to focus on 'those feelings both conscious and unconscious evoked in the worker by the task, context, organisational constraints and daily relationships' (Rustin, 2008, p. 4). Work discussion entails small, fixed groups of no more than eight in which each member brings a detailed written account of an interaction that captured their attention for whatever reason and that they wanted to think more about in the group. The purpose is to consider role, trying to understand what is being communicated both in the interaction and in the group when considering the account shared by the presenter. This helps to gain an enhanced understanding by engaging in the work discussion and using the group process to aid reflection and capture the experience.

This is a way to identify areas for further development, challenge preconceptions and open the discussion to perspectives beyond one's own. It can be a powerful experience, it has long been a part of psychoanalytically informed training and development and it is a well-established model in this respect. Foster (2020) evaluates its use beyond those taking a psychodynamic approach in her study concerning an adolescent PICU in which she details the benefits for participants who attended a work discussion group: 'positively impacted upon participant knowledge and understanding, emotion management, personal efficacy, therapeutic relationship building, managing challenging behaviour, leadership, professional identity and team cohesion' (p. 481).

Work discussion provides the opportunity in a supportive forum to consider interactions with colleagues, clients/patients and families to explore unconscious communication and dynamics and how they can influence care delivery and decision making. The focus is on thinking about the impacts and possible meanings of experiences. Rustin (2008) states that the aim is to sharpen perceptions and enable a richer understanding, a developing sensitivity, increased awareness and a degree of anxiety. Whilst this may seem counterintuitive, engagement with anxiety, and the ability to contain it, is a transferable skill required of practitioners working with complexity within teams and organisations, and this approach gives the opportunity to think about it away from the immediate care context.

Rustin (2008) goes on to say that coming to terms with the fact that there are no experts who can offer instant solutions is one problem that each participant must cope with to a degree. Other anticipated outcomes might be holding things in mind, learning to listen, appreciating the containing potential of setting and institution and thinking about what might be helpful alongside being realistic about what help is available (Rustin, 2008).

Understanding defence mechanisms

Defence mechanisms such as denial and avoidance are used by all of us and have their origins in our early attempts to cope with anxiety, abandonment, loss, conflict and emotional pain. As we develop, we are not immune to these unconscious attempts at keeping anxiety at bay, particularly in times of stress and anxiety. It therefore goes without saying that health and social care are fertile environments for this: 'Human service organisations are always going to be defensive against the possibility of overwhelming need' (Dartington, 2017, p. 174).

Given the everyday employment of defence mechanisms which Dartington (2017) says are essential because to focus on something, others must be put aside 'in the way that we close the door when we need to concentrate or want privacy; this becomes problematic only when we want to keep the door closed or locked' (p. 173); when this happens, defences can be over-relied on and become a problem. With this in mind, we advocate that being attentive to defence mechanisms that are an inevitable part of health and social care is crucial. In doing, practitioners can be supported through forums like work discussion, Schwartz rounds, Balint groups and reflective practice groups to think together. This has the potential to protect against the intrusion of defence mechanisms which turn the practitioner away from the primary task of providing high quality health and social care.

Conclusion

In this chapter, we have urged consideration of issues that can trouble those working in health and social care, particularly where the presentation of the service user seems difficult to understand and bear. In doing so, we proposed that Freud's (1914) 'Remembering, Repeating and Working Through' offers a framework through which these troubling experiences can be better understood. When that is achieved, it is likely that there will be less pressure to respond in defensive ways that try to protect the practitioner but that ultimately lead to ineffective care. This is frustrating for all involved, and worse, it risks setting up a dynamic where past difficulty such as abuse, rejection and humiliation are unthinkingly repeated.

Instead, we have suggested that a psychodynamic perspective can support the pursuit of high-quality health and social care given its focus on the concepts central to 'Remembering'. These include compulsion to repeat, transference, resistance and the impact of the unconscious. Through the example of a psychoanalytic reading group, we have shown the potential benefit in engaging in group discussion concerning a shared problem or experience. We extend this further to recommend engagement in facilitated reflective practice such as work discussion and Schwartz rounds with the aim of equipping practitioners with a solid foundation from which to manage the challenges of contemporary health and social care.

References

Abrahams, D. and Rohleder, P. (2021) *A Clinical Guide to Psychodynamic Psychotherapy*. London & New York. Routledge Taylor & Francis Group.

Ballatt, J., Campling, P. and Maloney, C. (2020) *Intelligent Kindness: Rehabilitating the Welfare State*. 2nd ed. Cambridge University Press.

BPC. https://www.bpc.org.uk/information-support/the-evidence-base/ Accessed 29th April 2025

Cardona, F. (2020) *Work Matters Consulting to Leader sand Organizations in the Tavistock Tradition*. London & New York. Routledge Taylor & Francis Group.

Dartington, T. (2017) The organisational context for good care in Vaspe, A. (ed.) *Psychoanalysis, The NHS, and Mental Health Work Today.* London. Karnac.

digital.nhs.uk. https://digital.nhs.uk/data-and-information/publications/statistical/nhs-talking-therapies-for-anxiety-and-depression-annual-reports/2022-23/therapy-based-outcomes# what-courses-of-therapy-are-patients-receiving Accessed 29th April 2025.

Fonagy, P. (2021) Forward in Abrahams, D. and Rohleder, P. (eds) *A Clinical Guide to Psychodynamic Psychotherapy.* London & New York. Routledge Taylor & Francis Group.

Foster, C. (2020) Investigating the impact of a psychoanalytic nursing development group within an adolescent psychiatric intensive care unit (PICU). *Archives of Psychiatric Nursing*, 34(6): 481–491.

Freud, S. (1914) Remembering, repeating and working through (further recommendations on the technique of psycho-analysis II) in *The Standard Edition of the Complete Psychological Works of Sigmund Freud*, Vol. 12, pp. 145–156. Hogarth Press and The Institute of Psychoanalysis.

Freud, S. (1923) *The Ego and the Id.* Standard Edition. 19.

King, P. (1978, Jan 1) Affective response of the analyst to the patient's communications. *The International Journal of Psycho-Analysis*, 59: 329–334.

Rustin, M. (2008) Work discussion: Some historical and theoretical observations in Rustin, M. and Bradley, J. (eds) *Work Discussion: Learning from Reflective Practice in Work with Children and Families.* London. Karnac Books.

Chapter 2

'Mourning and Melancholia' (Freud, 1917) in contemporary health and social care

Shelly Allen and Martin Gill

Introduction

In this chapter, we take 'Mourning and Melancholia' (Freud, 1917) as our focus. Freud's paper was published in 1917 but had been in development over a number of years; it is underpinned by the historical and cultural influences of the time and takes loss as its key theme. This is one of Freud's most famous and some would say influential papers, written at the time when Freud was moving from the predominance of the topographical model – based on the conscious, preconscious and unconscious – to the development of the structural model of the mind which sits alongside it – the id, ego and superego – as a way to understand and conceptualise the psyche. This can be traced in the paper, in which the ego features heavily and can be understood as our mostly conscious, rational self that mitigates between instinctual unconscious impulses and the desire for gratification driven by the id, with our conscience and moral code. This is referred to in 'Mourning' as critical agency, and Freud later termed it the superego.

Loss is an inherent part of our existence as humans, and what Freud brings into view in 'Mourning and Melancholia' is how we manage and fail to manage it. In the paper, Freud compares and contrasts mourning as a normal process associated with loss and grief with melancholia, which can loosely be thought of as a pervasive depression. Freud considers the 'mechanics' of these to illustrate the shared experiences and distinguishing features, but he urges caution, acknowledging that it is something of a work in progress, with some aspects more developed than others. What is clear though is that Freud's description of mourning remains relevant and contemporary. His insight into melancholia gives a framework for understanding why loss can become all encompassing and be felt personally beyond the grief reaction, as if the person is organised around it.

Freud's consideration of loss is in relation to a loved one but is extended to include other examples such as loss of one's country, liberty and an ideal. In this chapter, we take these key themes to encourage reflection on losses in their broadest sense and the responses to them, which can sometimes trouble those working in health and social care. The intention is to offer a framework for a deeper understanding of how and why someone can become stuck in relation to loss and the possible implications of this in the individual's presentation.

DOI: 10.4324/9781003541660-3

Case example

Freud's (1917) paper was the second we discussed in the psychoanalytically informed reading group introduced in Chapter 1. The group took the opportunity to discuss and reframe an understanding of mourning and melancholia/depression in light of Freud's proposal. The group considered depression as being predicated on an internal psychic vulnerability and thought about as a reaction both to and against loss and mourning. This then linked with the emergence of melancholia as a neurosis: a psychic defensive system which functions to defend the ego against unacceptable unconscious conflicts. This was further advanced through its relation to the capacity to bear mourning as a central developmental task but not one that is a given, as may often be assumed to be the case. Participants in the group were able to reflect on their experiences of working in NHS talking therapies and bereavement services where the task of mourning was anything but straightforward.

A developmental perspective was taken to elaborate on the internal psychic function and the action of depression in relation to experiences which create this situation. This allowed the group to begin to consider different ways to understand and think about these themes. Other aspects which the group were able to consider and resonated strongly with were thinking of depression through a lens of narcissism; the group felt this to be especially useful when thinking about the experiences of supporting service users. Themes such as countertransference, negative therapeutic reactions, suicidality and the clinical shift the patient needs to undertake to move from melancholia into mourning were considered in relation to the complication and complexity presented in 'Mourning'. One group member who worked within NHS talking therapies services brought a clinical example which helped to structure the discussion.

A female in late middle age had been referred to a bereavement service by her general practitioner. The service was staffed by counsellors who held a belief that the patient really needed to find a way to talk about her feelings and then something would change for the better. In introducing the woman's experience, the group member had already begun to shift in their views around mourning as a given and raised a question: can this woman find a way to mourn or are her psychic system and defences too well established to allow this to occur?

The woman described waiting at the window for her husband to return from work at the same time each day despite his death. The case was painful to hear and moved the group, and in the discussion and exploration, it came to light that the loss had in fact occurred many years previously, over ten years earlier. Clinically, the group member had been struggling, using techniques and support to gently challenge the prevailing belief as they saw it, but the task was really one of reality testing in bringing into view the loss that had occurred at least a decade earlier.

This allowed the group to return to 'Freud (1917)', which views the task of mourning in terms of reality testing: each memory comes back into view and in turn has to be mourned. This is a deeply painful psychic and emotional task, and during the discussion, once the gravity of the woman's defensive system became clear, the group was able to explore and consider the internal psychic actions which might have been at play in this situation. The group was able to wonder about the circumstances of the loss, the quality of the marital relationship prior to this and the patient's own psychic structures, particularly those related to self-regard. This discussion appeared to open something up, and the clinician began to add material to the discussion.

The patient's history was one of loss. Her father had died when she was around seven years old, and her sense was that her mother had never really got over this; she did not consider a further relationship and kept a shrine in the form of photographs of her husband through the ages which took centre stage in the family living room. At major life transitions, such as moving school, starting further education and the patient's wedding, her mother kept the lost husband/father alive for the family. It was possible to begin to establish links around identifications between the patient and her mother through loss and to consider what might be being defended against, such as rage, guilt and anger in relation to the death of their husband/father, all of which could be seen to have significantly complicated the task of mourning and led to a depressive solution against the pain associated with loss.

Although it was painful for the group to consider, especially the clinician whose case this was, links were formed between the paper and the complications of mourning and melancholia/depression and, further, how this might manifest for the individual, which allowed the group to consider the complexity of this. In turn, there was a shared appreciation of how this could complicate treatment and its progress, enabling a different perspective to be considered as a result.

Overview of the paper

As previously stated, 'Mourning and Melancholia' (Freud, 1917) is a far-reaching paper which has proven influential in how mourning and melancholia/depression are understood. In this paper, Freud offers a review of the similarities and differences between these, allowing the reader to gain connection with the central premise of the paper: how people manage loss or otherwise.

The mechanics of mourning are described as the ability to gradually divert the emotional energy in what or whom has been lost elsewhere. It is a conscious experience: the loss is known, and mourning is said to be complete when the reality of death can be faced. This allows the self a sense of freedom from the emotional labour of grief. In contrast to mourning, in melancholia, the loss of self-regard and esteem are evident. In identifying with the lost object which cannot be given up, it is taken in the self and becomes a target of self-reproach, seemingly with the belief that punishment is deserved. This links with Freud's reflections on suicide and mania, and despite the caveat in the paper that the concepts presented are a work in progress, 'Mourning' offers a formulation to consider suicidality from an intrapsychic position and deepen the understanding of this clinically.

Discussion

There are occasions when the presentation of a service user can be troubling, hard to understand and at times frustrating to those working in health and social care. The clinical example described above was typical of this where bereavement counselling was felt to have very little impact. Through the following discussion, we hope to offer a framework for supporting a deeper understanding of how and why loss impacts in a multitude of ways, and in so doing encourage a reflective stance when faced with its complexities. To begin with, we offer a context that underpins the point that loss is an inherent part of our existence and that early experiences can impact its management, or not, by taking a developmental perspective.

Loss, a developmental perspective

The thought of loss and death plagued Freud:

> I cannot face with comfort the idea of life without work, work and the free play of the imagination are for me the same thing, I take no pleasure in anything else. . . . Hence, in spite of all the acceptance of fate which is appropriate to an honest man, I have one quite secret prayer: that I may be spared any wasting away and crippling of my ability to work because of physical deterioration. In the words of King Macbeth, let us die in harness.
>
> (1910)

It is reasonable to suggest that there is a degree of familiarity with Freud's sentiment:

> to fear death is not the same as to recognise its inevitability, which is a fact forced on us much against our will by the repeated experience that no good (or bad) experience can ever last for ever – a fact perhaps never fully accepted.
>
> (Money-Kyrle, 2015, p. 231)

As such, it is not unusual to be apprehensive in relation to changes as we age and to wonder about death, although we also want to propose that loss is inherent no matter how difficult it may be to face.

Piontelli (1992) undertook a study of pre-natal life accessed through the ultrasound scans of 11 growing foetuses from around the 16th week of pregnancy to explore their pre-natal lives. She then observed the babies as closely as possible after birth on a weekly basis until they were one year old. This continued monthly until two years of age and then two or three times a year until the child was four, with consistencies being noted in the pre- and post-natal period. The author concluded from the findings that the interplay between nature and nurture begins much earlier than previously thought.

Piontelli's (1992) recordings of observable behaviour illustrated continuity between the foetus and the infant once born into childhood. From this point, it is not a great leap to appreciate how a baby's movement from the pre-natal environment – if in Winnicott's term it is 'good enough' and a safe, cosseted place where the warmth and nutrition required to grow and develop are provided without the need to ask – to its post-natal world through birth, characterised by the infant's scream for survival and dependency on others, can be experienced and thought of as a loss. The experience of birth is always an extremely important event, and whilst it is unlikely to be remembered, it is relived and reworked as the child grows (Piontelli, 1992).

Developmentally, this loss is understood not cognitively but bodily and is supported by Freud's (1923) statement that 'the ego is first and foremost a bodily ego' (p. 26); developmental loss continues. For instance, weaning occurs during a limited period in the baby's first year and becomes a prototype for all separations and losses (Waddell, 2002) and is evoked throughout the crucial period of adolescence. Copley (1993) describes how the adolescent process signifies the movement from the mentality of childhood to adulthood where dependence on external parents gradually ends (Copley, 1993). The significance of this is illustrated by Waddell (2002), who states that adolescence can be seen as a complex adjustment to the major physical and emotional changes brought about during puberty. Bodily changes occur more rapidly during puberty than at any other period of life except in the womb. Given that physiological changes tend to occur earlier than emotional ones, these changes are accompanied by psychological upheaval (Waddell, 2002).

Waddell (2002) goes on to argue that the manageability of the associated disturbances is dependent on the quality of containment as an infant, the degree of stability enjoyed during latency around ages 6–12 and the internal and external pressures contended with by the young person. The negotiation of the relationship between child and adulthood, the transition from life in the family to life in the world, finding and establishing an identity – including a sexual identity – all encompass the capacity to manage separation, loss, choice, independence and possibly disillusionment with life (Waddell, 2002), and the tasks of adolescence concern all these.

Having to give up external figures of attachment and dependence and to internalise them as resources in the development of the personality involves mourning and loss (Waddell, 2002). These are inherent, and as Polmear (2004) contends, the relationship with the mother of the two-year-old self must be rescinded so the adolescent can embark on a relationship with the mother of their present. Failure during adolescence to separate internally from the parents of one's childhood impacts on more pervasive emotional difficulties in adult relationships; examples include feeling stuck in a deadlock, seemingly making the move from child to adult but only in an inauthentic way (Polmear, 2004). This can be thought about in relation to the case example described earlier and in particular the clinical example of not being able to mourn loss and being stuck in this state of melancholia. This will be developed further using vignettes to follow.

Much has been written from a psychoanalytic perspective regarding adolescence but less about mid-life. By the age of around 50, a person might be regarded as a grown-up, by both the self and by others (Waddell, 2002), and potentially there is much to enjoy, but there is also 'midlife's psychic work' to navigate (Montero, de Montero & de Vogelfanger, 2013, p. xvii). A midlife crisis is a familiar concept in the Global North, but we propose that in the period since this text was published in 2013, the way in which a midlife crisis may manifest has changed.

The Independent newspaper in the UK ran an article on 7th April 2025 discussing the previously understood signs of a midlife crisis, such as buying a sports car or embarking on relationships with younger partners, as past tense. Typically, this crisis is now said to manifest as hair transplants, gruelling fitness regimes, retreats and relying on sleep technology to get a good night's rest, all of which are considered indicative of the millennial midlife crisis. From a psychodynamic perspective, this can be understood as taking action to try to deny the inevitable ageing process, to use defence mechanisms to ward off the progress of time towards older age and thereby finish where this section began: with Freud's trepidation.

Having offered a perspective as to why loss is an inherent part of being human, we urge consideration of it when working with people who access health and social care services. Having a developmental perspective that appreciates loss, mourning and the potential for melancholia enables taking up a more informed stance. We will now focus on specific examples that will be familiar to those working in health and social care.

Moving on in therapeutic settings

Health and social care is finite; there is not enough provision to satisfy need, and concerns about this in individual workers, teams and institutions can translate into a fear of being overwhelmed. This point was made by Dartington (2017), who stated that organisations that provide a human service are pushed into being defensive because there is always more that can be done.

Defensive manoeuvres in this respect might include denial that a person's needs are sufficient to meet the threshold for intervention. Disavowed by concluding it is the fault of the individual, they use drugs, they are violent and aggressive, despite having needs that the service is tasked to address. A common complaint made by workers is that the service user is getting 'too dependent', sometimes resulting in a withdrawal of care and attention.

Where contact has been made with health and social care provision, it is reasonable to suggest that there is hope – whether conscious or unconscious – that something might be provided to relieve whatever has prompted contact. When this hope is quashed, it is conceivable that it is felt as a loss, and some losses can be borne, and some losses are shattering. It is hard to know how an individual might experience this unless it is routinely thought and/or enquired about. To illustrate this, a vignette is presented once the context to it is set.

Forensic services care for people who have mental health problems and have also committed criminal offences; they are tasked to provide a therapeutic and secure environment to maintain public safety. Some who are receiving treatment, once deemed to have improved, will be returned to prison to complete the rest of their sentence as dictated by the courts. Others are deemed unable to take legal responsibility for the offences in the same way, and rather than going to prison, they are directed by the court to be admitted to a secure unit for care and treatment of their mental health condition, with a view to rehabilitation.

Once recovered and rehabilitated, those who have committed violent crimes whilst under the influence of their mental disorder may live in the community whilst being monitored by the mental health team involved in their care. Legally, this includes the right to recall individuals to the secure unit should there be concerns about a deterioration in mental state, this being deemed in their best interests and for the safety of the public.

Working in a locked clinical area providing admission and assessment within a forensic unit, I have experiences of people being recalled to the unit. In the time I worked in this area, I do not remember a bed ever being free, and recalling involved moving other people around to make space. This would begin with reviewing who in the rehabilitation area could be discharged with support to live in the community or at least go on long-term home leave. Making the decision freed up space for the best candidate within the locked area to move on and relinquish their place to make way for the new/old arrival.

Looking down the list and identifying who could be moved was often done in a pressured state, as if the safety of the community depended on the speed at which this could be arranged. To an extent, this might have been valid, but it also speaks of a lack of opportunity to stop and think it through. The speed with which these decisions were made could be experienced as an accolade for decisive and strong leadership, but what of the person being moved?

I do not recall any depth of thought to a degree I now feel is warranted being afforded to the impact of this move on the 'chosen' person, other than to present the decision as progress. Moving on to a more open setting, albeit within the confines of a locked service, was declared to be a good thing. However, the chosen person may have spent a great deal of time in this clinical area as is typical within forensic services, working with these members of staff and sharing a living space with those also in receipt of care and so developing relationships, albeit in a somewhat strange environment. Moving from being deemed acutely disturbed to being ready for rehabilitation can be something to celebrate, but with no space to consider the losses as a result. Cardona (2020) refers to this as a culture of 'positiveness' which can be understood as a shield against negative projections and can become a barrier to being psychologically present. The ability to experience the loss, if indeed this was how it was felt, and to mourn, was negated by the practical, no-nonsense requirement to move on whether the person felt prepared or not.

Vignette

Stefan was well known to the service; he had been admitted to the forensic unit having committed a violent offence and had a diagnosis of schizophrenia. He was a white male from a middle-class background who had started to experience psychosis as a university student living away from home. He had been described as bright, a very good student, he and others had shared aspirations for his future. When Stefan attracted the notice of health services, he was able to give a good account of himself, and therefore, care and intervention were delayed, and his psychosis deteriorated. Stefan's index offence, the event that brought him into contact with the criminal justice and health services, was violent and sustained, provoked by paranoia and suspicion that he was to come to grave harm if he did not defend himself first.

Stefan had spent a significant amount of time in the assessment and admission unit. He was described as quiet and polite in his interactions; he mostly kept himself to himself but enjoyed chess and talking about music with staff, and he had relationships. Over the preceding weeks, he had been given an increasing level of independence, such as no longer being escorted to the dining room for meals by a member of staff and attending occupational health classes without a nurse. Outwardly things seemed to be going well. When a bed needed to be found due to recalling a patient from the community, Stefan was considered the best candidate to move to the rehabilitation area.

However, after a few weeks, Stefan's distress became apparent when this was not put into words but acted out instead. He used a drink can that he had bought from the onsite vending machine to cut himself and to threaten staff should they enter his room. Stefan eventually allowed staff support, but not before he made a series of cuts to his arm which necessitated treatment. In hindsight, one hypothesis might be that the opinion of clinical staff, stressing the positive of moving to a more independent area and having more freedom, conflicted with Stefan's experience of spending more time alone, losing the connections he previously had and rupturing relationships he had previously forged – put briefly, a loss. Freud (1917) makes a link between the development of melancholia and other losses that have not been effectively mourned. Loss of Stefan's future self, the regard of his parents, who seldom visited, and his liberty as a consequence of his mental health issues and offences were all relevant here.

In 'Mourning and Melancholia', the depressed patient internalises the original object (the parent) as a way of avoiding the pain of separation and loss. The object becomes part of the person's mind where it is criticised and attacked for failing to be ideal (Evans, 2021). An appreciation of the devastation that Stefan's mental health issues and offending behaviour had on his development and aspirations for the future, felt by him and his parents, – who were also invested in this – links here and is captured in one of Freud's famous quotes from the paper.

> Thus the shadow of the object fell upon the ego and the latter could henceforth be judged by a special agency, as though it were an object, the forsaken object.
>
> (1917, p. 249).

Freud states that the main difference between mourning and melancholia is the presence of self-denigration in the latter: it is the world that has become poor and empty in mourning, whilst it is the ego itself in melancholia. Returning to the notion of loss in its broadest sense as described by Freud, perhaps another aspect of the dynamic was that it was more manageable for Stefan to remain 'disturbed' rather than progressing and having to face the offence and his mental health issues in a reality-oriented way. Evans (2021) states that when patients become aware of the extent of their difficulties, they have to face up to anxiety, loss and despair and may be prone to feelings of humiliation, and this is relevant in relation to suicidal actions. Evans states that in melancholia, aggression is directed towards the self and away from the external object that has failed them.

When Stefan returned to the assessment and admission unit due to the incident just described, relationships were re-established; he took up his previous interests and future moves were considered in relation to what had happened previously. However, it may be reasonable to suggest that had a psychodynamic position been taken up before Stefan's move, perhaps the turbulence that was evoked could have been anticipated, and more thought given to how Stefan could be helped to manage all that this stirred up for him.

Attention to endings and loss in therapy is a crucial part of the process, yet despite Stefan developing significant relationships with clinical staff, this was not at the forefront of consideration about moving him to a different clinical area. We propose that this was a missed opportunity for appreciating the gravity of loss if it is not attended to sufficiently and that this then impacts the experience of care and support. It also seems reasonable to reflect on the case example here where discussion of Freud (1917) in relation to what resonated with the group and applied through the clinical example illustrated this point where a change in perspective was gained.

Moving on in educational settings

Whilst a different type of relationship exists in educational rather than therapeutic settings, we propose these are often hugely meaningful. Many people can recall a standout teacher from school or college, and for those who attended university, role models who inspire future aspiration and direction may be recalled with appreciation. Yet the significance of endings as students complete their studies seldom gets thought about beyond the celebration. This echoes Stefan's experience and Cardona's comments regarding the culture of positiveness (Cardona, 2020).

The significance of educational settings was aptly described by Polmear (1993):

There is something very special about the educational setting which makes it in one way similar to the analytic one: in its explicit offer of what I call developmental hope. . . . There is an excitement and hope inherent in growing up which is mirrored in the analysand's approach to his analyst as he sets out on his analytic journey. . . . I am suggesting, in the educational setting too is for an experience which will transform the self.

(p. 242)

It is undoubtedly true that education can be transformative; perhaps this can be described as a default position. It is an expectation that it will lead to opportunities for growth and development alongside the fulfilment of aspirations. However, there are also occasions where something seems to have become stuck. In a similar way to the constant reminders in the form of photographs brought into significant life events in the clinical example, metaphorically, an incomplete course may perform a similar function, an inability to move on and face reality. We advance this point with the following vignette.

Vignette

Valerie had gained indefinite leave to remain in the UK after successfully seeking asylum. She was living in the UK without family who had remained at home and was trying to make a life for herself. Valerie had been a trainee solicitor, but this was not an option available to her in the UK. After gaining work as a nursing assistant and successfully completing an access course to higher education, Valerie had started an undergraduate degree leading to registration as a mental health nurse.

Valerie progressed well until her third year, when she failed her final assignment twice. Ordinarily, this would mean that Valerie would be withdrawn from the programme for having failed to complete the required assignments. However, she was able to use the mitigating circumstance process aimed at supporting students who had encountered personal difficulties which had impaired their ability to pass. Due to this, Valerie was offered an additional attempt which she also failed. This led Valerie to appeal on the basis that the situation impairing her second attempt was ongoing and had not resolved. It was noted by the programme team that until this point, Valerie had progressed without difficulty, but there seemed to be something getting in the way of passing her final assignment, which would mean completing the course, leaving university and being eligible to register as a nurse.

At one level, this was understood as the anxiety which often accompanies students as they complete their preparation for professionally registered programmes. Moving from the relative security of student status with university and placement support is usually anxiety provoking. However, it was only when the full context of Valerie's experiences were thought about that its true impact could be appreciated. Leaving all that Valerie had known including her formative, significant relationships, albeit in a volatile and frightening set of circumstances, to move across the globe needed to be held in mind. Having forged new relationships that would change with leaving university and starting full time employment, this turned out to be very difficult to bear. It was hypothesised that this situation stirred up all previous loss that Valerie had not mourned. Once this was better understood in the context of transference, with Valerie displacing her expectations and feelings relating to past formative relationships onto her current circumstances, support could be tailored to allow Valerie to complete the course.

It is not only relationships with people that can evoke an emotional response: transference can also be felt in relation to organisations. I could have started my clinical training in psychotherapy in my home city. Instead, I returned to where I had studied before, even though all the tutors on my clinical course were different to those I had studied with previously. I understood this as an attachment to the organisation and what it represented for me, and I am not alone in this.

Relating to organisations and institutions

It is not only with people that deep relationships can develop; organisations and institutions can also hold a place of significance, and loss can be felt beyond interpersonal relationships: 'Mourning is regularly the reaction to the loss of a loved person, or to the loss of some abstraction which has taken the place of one, such as one's country, liberty, and ideal and so on' (Freud, 1917, p. 243).

As we will illustrate, an appreciation of this can help understand what may otherwise be dismissed and diminished.

Vignette

Peter was in his sixties and one of the first patients to be admitted to a forensic clinic that became regarded as a centre of excellence. It was progressive in terms of its therapeutic approach, and Peter had been a high-profile case when he committed his index offence and was admitted. He progressed well with care and therapeutic intervention to the point of discharge to live in the community after a number of years of in-patient treatment.

Peter was someone whose legal status meant he could be recalled back into hospital should his mental state deteriorate because of its link to his violent offending. He was closely monitored by the community team attached to the clinic and was maintained in the neighbourhood where he had settled. However, later in Peter's rehabilitation, a new pattern emerged whereby just before Christmas, Peter would disturb his community team to such an extent that he was recalled back into hospital. One year, he decided to by-pass this process and arrived at the clinic door with his case packed, ready for admission.

The staff group at the clinic were both the same and different; some had moved on since its opening, and others had joined. On reflection, it did not seem to be just the staff members who drew Peter back at such a significant time of year. For some, it was a standing joke that Peter was getting ready for his Christmas dinner, but engagement, with the possible meaning of Peter's actions offers additional perspectives. If this was the place he felt compelled to be, it calls into question of why there of all places.

Again, it draws attention to being stuck and not being able to bear loss; in Peter's case, this could have been linked to his status as an early resident in a centre of excellence, and at that time, a man to be feared by others. It is also significant that the pattern of Christmas recall, aligned with his advancing age led to the hypothesis that admission was an antidote against loneliness and all the loss Peter had experienced, which he could not bear to mourn.

The use of the organisation in this respect can be thought of in relation to containment (Bion, 1963). Cardona (2020, p. 23) describes organisational containment as 'the idea that organizations should provide a safe environment where people could feel held and "contained"'. A reasonable understanding of this situation is that Peter's desire to be cared for, consciously and/or unconsciously, drew him back to the unit, where there was an absence of personal, sustaining relationships beyond those with his mental health team supporting him in the community, who would be away from work due to the time of year. One hypothesis is that the organisation itself was being called upon to perform that function. This potentially offered a deeper understanding of the dynamics at play, and whilst a Christmas dinner was no doubt welcome, it is possible to see the function of the organisation as providing so much more.

Implications and recommendations

A psychodynamic orientation

Through the case example and vignettes, we have shown how a psychodynamic approach to the work of health and social care can open different perspectives, this is something Britton (2004) talked about in terms of a triangular space. This is achieved by taking up the position of a self-observer when working with patients in a psychoanalytically informed way. Developmentally, it relates to how we gain the ability to take in different perspectives to our own. This can be tracked in the discussion relating to the reading group and the vignettes.

This can be supported by those trained in a psychodynamic/analytic modality, as we have illustrated in this chapter. Psychodynamic approaches to supervision, case discussion, reading groups and work discussion should not be confined to those undergoing this type of training. The complexities in health and social care warrant a space where the conscious and unconscious processes can be thought about. We have shown how this benefited a reading group which consisted of psychological practitioners, psychotherapists, undergraduate and postgraduate students and university staff. We have also shown how a deeper appreciation of the key issues was gained which could be taken forward in relation to understanding the complexities of loss, mourning and melancholia within health and social care.

Loss as a given not just an event

We stress the need to see loss in its broadest sense through an appreciation of its inherent presence in psychic life. Using a developmental perspective offers a framework for supporting curiosity about what is being experienced as loss and mourned effectively or otherwise.

We stress that loss is ubiquitous, it is not confined to those accessing services to receive health and social care. It is experienced in the practitioners delivering care and evoked anywhere where relationships are forged such as in educational settings when preparing to become health and social care professionals. Appreciating this may therefore facilitate curiosity about loss as an inherent part of the dynamic; in turn the similarities and differences between mourning and melancholia might help to ensure that loss in its broadest sense can be thought about when considering people's experiences.

Remembering to consider 'Who are you?'

The introduction stressed a way of keeping in mind the similarities and differences in encounters through health and social care. We include it here as a way of reiterating the importance of taking an intersectional approach that acknowledges loss of loved ones, of liberty, of country and ideals as encouraged by Freud (1917). Tummala-Narra (2020) urges the need to hold in mind immigrants' multiple identities which risk becoming invisible due to racism and stereotyping. We think keeping the question 'Who are you?' (Belkin, 2020, p. 7) in mind serves as a reminder not to dismiss difference in the face of similarity, and as Britton (2004) stressed, taking up a triangular space that is open to perspectives beyond one's own.

Conclusion

Through an overview of the paper, applied case example and vignettes, we have shown how 'Mourning and Melancholia' (Freud, 1917) offers a framework to consider loss in its broadest sense. We urge consideration of this in relation to Belkin's 'Who are you?' (2020, p. 7) so that an appreciation of this nuanced and unique experience can be held in mind by those tasked to support people through health and social care.

Loss is susceptible to denial, but we urge approaches that are reality oriented which can take account of conscious and unconscious processes to help bear the impact of this. We have shown how a psychodynamic perspective offers much in this respect and can be applied to a range of settings which support health and social care. This includes clinical and educational provision where practitioners and educators are not necessarily familiar with or trained in psychodynamic approaches. In so doing, an understanding of the impact of loss and its management or otherwise, through mourning and melancholia, can be thought about and supported.

References

Belkin, M. (2020) Who is queer around here? Overcoming rigid thinking and relating in patient and analyst in Belkin, M., & White, C. (eds) *Intersectionality and Relational Psychoanalysis*. London & New York. Routledge Taylor & Francis Group.

Bion, W.R. (1963) *Elements of Psychoanalysis*. London. Heinemann.

Britton, R. (2004) *Sex, Death, and the Superego Experiences in Psychoanalysis*. London & New York. Karnac.

Cardona, F. (2020) *Work Matters Consulting to Leader sand Organizations in the Tavistock Tradition*. London & New York. Routledge Taylor & Francis Group.

Copley, B. (1993) Adolescence a process of change in *The World of Adolescence. Literature, Society and Psychoanalytic Psychotherapy*. London. Free association Books.

Dartington, T. (2017) The organisational context for good care in Vaspe, A. (ed.) *Psychoanalysis, the NHS, and Mental Health Work Today*. London. Karnac.

Evans, M. (2021) *Psychoanalytic Thinking in Mental Health Settings*. London & New York. Routledge Taylor & Francis Group.

Freud, S. (1910) In a letter to Oskar Pfister, 6th March 1910. https://www.freud.org.uk/2018/10/30/freud-and-the-later-life/ accessed 29th April 2025.

Freud, S. (1917) Mourning and melancholia in *The Standard Edition of the Complete Psychological Works of Sigmund Freud, Volume XIV (1914–1916): On the History of the Psycho-Analytic Movement, Papers on Metapsychology and Other Works*, 237–258.

Freud, S. (1923) *The Ego and the Id*. Standard Edition. 19.

Money-Kyrle, R. (2015) *Man's Picture of His World and Three Papers* (ed.) Harris Williams. M. London. Karnac.

Montero, G.J., de Montero, A.M.C., & de Vogelfanger, L.S. (2013) *Updating Midlife: Psychoanalytic Perspectives*. First edition. London. Karnac Books.

Piontelli, A. (1992) *From Fetus to Child an Observational and Psychoanalytic Study*. East Sussex. Routledge.

Polmear, C. (1993) Beginnings and endings: Therapeutic opportunities in educational settings. *Psychoanalytic Psychotherapy*, Vol. 7, No. 3, 241–251.

Polmear, C. (2004) Dying to live: Mourning, melancholia and the adolescent process. *Journal of Child Psychotherapy*, Vol. 30, No. 3, 263–274.

The Independent. (2025) https://www.independent.co.uk/life-style/millennial-midlife-crisis-signs-b2726788.html accessed 29th April 2025.

Tummala-Narra, P. (2020) Intersectionality in the immigrant context in Belkin, M., & White, C. *Intersectionality and Relational Psychoanalysis*. London & New York. Routledge Taylor & Francis Group.

Waddell, M. (2002) *Inside Lives Psychoanalysis and the Growth of the Personality*. London. Karnac.

Chapter 3

Making space in health and social care for 'Hate in the Counter-Transference' (Winnicott, 1949)

Shelly Allen

Introduction

The aim of this chapter is to instil in the reader the importance of safe spaces to help work through the inevitably challenging experiences that are evoked when working in health and social care. The health and social care professions predominantly attract those who are motivated to attend to others. These professionals are likely to feel compassion, empathy and at times, identification with the person and the issues which have led to contact with services.

In thoughtful settings, it is acceptable to share these feelings as a way of managing their impact on staff. In some ways, they reinforce that the personal attributes, attitude and motivation to offer high-quality, personalised care is evident, and the associated need to support health and social care practitioners to avoid compassion fatigue is well documented.

What tends to attract less attention in contemporary health and social care settings are feelings that may seem counter to the motivation to help and care. Those associated with the stresses and strain of what it is to be overwhelmed, to feel disgust, repulsion and contempt. Such feelings seemingly have no place in the competent, caring professional, yet they play a part in the everyday experiences of what it is to work in health and social care.

Where feelings associated with hatred are intolerable in the staff member, they may lead to reliance on defence mechanisms which are unconsciously employed to try to manage what is stirred up in the worker. Typically, these might include denial of hatred and avoidance of the source for this. This may translate into observable action such as minimising the issues experienced by the person using the service or blaming them for needing input. Becoming task orientated and privileging activity which keeps a distance from the person such as giving undue attention to administrative tasks.

Using residential settings for people who are experiencing disturbing mental health problems as an example, there are many ways that making a connection with people using the service can be interrupted by such tasks, for instance, leaving someone to wait for something because the worker who has been asked for assistance, is doing the observations. These are timed checks to maintain safety, which are then documented as a record of what the person is doing and how they appear.

DOI: 10.4324/9781003541660-4

It is undeniable that such tasks are important, but where this activity takes precedence over direct contact with a person who needs assistance, and is at the expense of personalised support, it warrants thoughtful attention. Such fleeting contact enables superficiality whilst performing care-related tasks. Further consideration of this offers an opportunity to think about what is getting in the way of fulfilling the person's request. This can be thought of as a hypothesis, a possible explanation for what might be happening rather than definitive and absolute.

Perhaps doing the observations is a way of intermittently checking in but not engaging with those who are experiencing distress. Perhaps it allows avoidance of painful feelings in the worker which could be evoked if a more attentive understanding of the person's experiences and needs were gained. Maybe there is an indirect message to the rest of the team, highlighting their need to respond to the request for assistance; perhaps the staff member doing the observations feels they are the only one engaged in work.

Where the nature of the work and what gets evoked is painful and difficult, a psychodynamic approach can encourage consideration beyond the superficial to gain a deeper understanding. When this is achieved, a more informed position and choice might be possible. The importance of this is that it may reduce the pull towards acting out, which is a way of indirectly managing a feeling through action because it cannot be thought about (Lemma, 2016).

Acting out and reliance on defence mechanisms such as avoidance and denial are more likely if a safe, supportive place to think about the impact of the work is not available, such as leaving the person waiting whilst saying 'I can't unlock the kitchen for you, I'm doing *the* observations' is one example of this.

In contrast, the opportunity to have a safe space to consider the impact of the work can help in working through them and possibly resolving some of the difficulties through a shared, open understanding. The need for such a thoughtful, considered approach prompted Donald Winnicott to write his paper 'Hate in the Countertransference', published in 1949.

In this paper, Winnicott offers the importance of transparency for encouraging open dialogue with oneself and others. The purpose being so that these difficult, disturbing reactions might have the chance to be worked through and processed. thereby reducing their negative impact on the relationship, work and outcome for the service user. This chapter aims to encourage a reflective, thoughtful stance to the work of health and social care. This will be organised around acknowledgement of the inherent challenges posed by the contemporary context of care. It will be progressed through consideration of the impact this may have on practitioners, groups, teams and the overall organisation, which in turn influences the way in which an individual experiences the support offered and the care delivered.

I encourage you to reflect on your experiences, prompted by the everyday examples used in the chapter, and to consider the importance of engendering an open approach with trusted others, the purpose being an attempt to prevent unwanted aspects of the dynamic between practitioner and service user, from negatively intruding and disrupting the work. In doing, the primary task, that which an organisation must perform if it is to survive (Rice, 1963), in this context high-quality health and social care which is effective and acceptable to those in receipt of it, could be enabled.

In considering hate within the context of this chapter, it is the feelings of intense dislike, disgust, aversion, contempt and even aggression that may manifest in what is said. How it is said or even not said, and how it is experienced by the other, that is the focus here. Whilst this may feel contradictory to providing high-quality, personalised, integrated health and social care, as the following discussion will propose, its acknowledgement is imperative for meeting this primary task.

Whilst hate is familiar, the concept of countertransference may be less so. Initially, Freud viewed countertransference as an obstacle to the therapeutic endeavour between patient and psychoanalyst/therapist. Further development since Freud's initial misgivings means that it is considered a given in therapeutic relationships with widespread acknowledgement that if attended to, this can be a valuable source of information enabling the therapist to connect with the inner world of the patient and their interpersonal experiences. Put succinctly, 'Countertransference is made up of our responses to the patient's material, including feelings, thoughts and behaviour in relation to the patient' (Abrahams & Rohleder, 2021, p. 196).

An example may be feeling a connection with someone, linking to feelings of warmth and prompting the desire to help and assist them going above and beyond what one might usually be expected to provide. Conversely, the feelings stirred up may prompt rejection and avoidance of the person, a desire not to be connected to something troubling and unsettling. These examples illustrate how feelings and thoughts may lead to particular actions. If this remains outside of self-awareness, it risks impacting the ability to remain resourceful, supportive and curious about the person's circumstances, and in this situation, the primary task is undermined.

Therapists undergo in-depth training and personal therapy to use countertransference in their work; as such, I am not advocating the use of this without due regard. However, countertransference is not confined to the therapy relationship; it is an everyday experience wherever relationships exist. Extending an understanding of this concept beyond those who are trained in psychodynamic theory enables an understanding of the dynamics between health and social care practitioners and those who use services, in an informed way. This enables reflective practice and is different from the way a therapist would use their countertransference to propose a hypothesis about the person's experiences.

Countertransference as an aspect of reflective practice can therefore be used to enable a safe, what Winnicott referred to as a '"holding" environment' and when not attended to, what gets stirred up in the practitioner could illustrate Freud's early misgivings concerning countertransference. Protection against this requires a safe space where reactions and response can be worked through and processed, guarding against an unwanted impact on the work, as will be discussed later in this chapter. It is in stating the importance of this here that the following critique may be addressed: 'too often, the attention of educators, managers and staff is directed to the technical, the performative elements of the clinical or caring task, rather than the relational' (Ballatt, Campling & Maloney, 2020, p. 37). To progress this further, a case example will be outlined.

Case example

David identified as a black man; he had been admitted to secure forensic provision for assessment of his mental health, which at the time was said to have deteriorated in prison. The reason given for this was that David had become the target for aggression and acts of violence, to the point that he was expressing suicidal ideation. David had a history of non-violent acquisitive offences, which was contrary to the rest of the male patient population he was living with at that time whose index offences, those that had brought them to the attention of the criminal justice and mental health service involved aggressive acts perpetrated against others.

David was unpopular with other patients; they described him in ways that can be summarised as intrusive and irritating, an example being changing the television channel whilst others were watching it or switching it on and increasing the volume at night when others were trying to sleep. He seemed to have a knack of saying and doing the wrong thing, and he did not fit in; he was not invited to the gym by other patients, was not included in the group order for takeaways at the weekend and ate alone in the dining room. His relationships with staff members were largely of a similar pattern. No one volunteered to go for a walk with him or escort him to meals; the nurse in charge would assign someone to do this, and at mealtimes, the staff member would often sit away from him in the coffee area with other staff, the rationale being David preferred it that way.

During David's assessment, it was concluded that his mental health issues were not a significant contributory factor in his offending history, and as such, he should be dealt with by the criminal justice system. The further complication with this was that David was residing in the country illegally, and it was decided that he should be deported to his country of origin. At that time, this area was politically unstable, violent and undergoing much upheaval.

The day that David was transferred from the unit back to prison, there was a collective sense of relief; television could now be enjoyed uninterrupted, sleep would be restful and jokes were made at David's expense. Within the staff group, there was no discussion or sense of engagement with the likely horror of being returned to a war-torn country with all the issues that David took with him. Reflecting back, there was very little sense of curiosity in relation to how David communicated through his manner and actions or how those who had committed horrendous crimes seemed to be more acceptable and easier to be with.

A safe supportive space to more fully consider the impact of David and how he presented was not available at that time, and whilst it is unlikely to have changed the outcome for David in terms of being moved on, it may have enabled words to be put to this difficult dynamic and a place to consider what was driving David to present in this way. Importantly, what might have been hypothesised to prompt a better understanding and a way of being with him that did not replicate the rejection and dismissal he had experienced in his earlier life. It is here that Winnicott (1949) offers detail in understanding the complexity of hate in the context of therapeutic relationships.

Overview of the paper

The importance of being open to disturbing feelings and having a place to talk about them so they do not interfere with the work prompted Donald Winnicott to write his essay on hate which later became the paper entitled 'Hate in the Counter-Transference'. Despite this, it was not popularly acclaimed; in contrast to other papers written by Winnicott, which had typically become 'instant classics', this essay received a 'frosty reception' (Kahr, 2014, p. 70).

In the paper, Winnicott (1949) refers to hate in the countertransference as an aspect of ambivalence. This can be thought of as holding contradictory feeling states in the relationship towards one object, an object being the mental and emotional image taken into the self (Bott Spillius et al., 2011). An example of this is the internal representation of primary caregivers which evokes both loving and hateful feelings.

Related to this, Winnicott says that working therapeutically with 'psychotics' is impossible unless the analyst is aware of their own hate to prevent it intruding in the work. Gabbard (1994) clarifies that Winnicott's 'psychotics' were those who were later diagnosed with a personality disorder. Whilst this is a contested psychiatric diagnosis, the examples of these mechanisms briefly described are likely to feel familiar to those working in health and social care both in relation to staff and service users, whether the diagnostic classification is accepted or not.

Winnicott goes on to say that the ideas proposed in the paper are relevant beyond those who take a psychoanalytic approach. In this, it is stressed that however much love there may be for patients, this does not offer protection from hating and fearing them. Further, the better this is known, the less chance hate and fear will impact.

In focusing on "psychotics", Winnicott refers to an environmental failure in early life, this being related to the experiences of being cared for from birth by parents and significant others. Winnicott goes on to contrast these environmental failures with the holding environment provided by the analyst. This train of thought is progressed with what would now be considered the unconventional approach of supporting a nine-year-old boy who had been in residential care: 'he was the most lovable and most maddening of children' (Winnicott, 1949, p. 354) who was taken into Winnicott's home to be cared for over a period of three months. Through this experience, Winnicott demonstrated the importance of making hate conscious to ensure it did not manifest in unconscious ways.

To progress this point, Winnicott details all the ways in which the mother hates her baby, and whilst this may be difficult to embrace, these examples may be familiar. These include that the baby may be a risk to the mother during pregnancy and birth, causes pain during breastfeeding, is ruthless and treats her like an unpaid servant and at first, the baby does not know what the mother does and sacrifices for them. Winnicott highlights the importance of this saying, much as with the nine-year-old boy, that the mother must tolerate hating her baby without doing anything about it. This point was extended in Winnicott's paper to the challenge of treating 'insane' people. It is observed that the cruel treatment of people who were experiencing mental distress may be explained due to the hatred of patients experienced by mental health professionals. This, like Winnicott's proposal in terms of the mother's feelings towards her baby, was highly controversial and unwelcome.

It is in summarising these main points from Winnicott (1949) that a greater appreciation may be gained of the lukewarm reception to this paper. Although, it also speaks to the task of being able to tolerate feelings of hate without doing anything about them. As such, it is reasonable to state that acknowledging hate in the countertransference can be therapeutic, much in the same way that it is now more acceptable to acknowledge the impact and disturbance of being a primary carer for a baby, even if not endorsed wholesale.

This ground-breaking proposal not only stressed the importance of the holding environment as a healing factor in therapy. It also led to a shift in understanding countertransference, which moved from Freud's initial misgivings that it was an interference to treatment to the normalization of hateful feelings between the clinician and patient (Gabbard, 1994).

Discussion

The notion that hate may feature in the work of health and social care practitioners could be said to present a complexity which would rather be denied. The case example of David is an illustration of this. The impact that David had on others and the responses he was subject to were not given the opportunity to be thought through. The lack of a supportive space for staff to be able to think more clearly meant the opportunity to do something different for David whilst he was on the unit was not available; if it had been, perhaps a more comprehensive understanding could have been achieved. As it is, what is left is the feeling that David was misunderstood, a target for others' hatred and violence, a scapegoat for issues which did not fully belong to him, and as a result, a sponge to soak up feelings of hate that could not be talked about.

Reviewing the professional standards of key health and social care regulators such as the Nursing & Midwifery Council, Social Work England and the Health Care Professions Council, it may be reasonable to suggest that disclosures of hate are highly concerning. Yet where trusted relationships are forged, and hate can be acknowledged, it is clear that they not only exist but can be modified through time and space with trusted colleagues. In encouraging engagement in these experiences and providing a containing presence, trusted colleagues can help reduce the likelihood of a negative impact on the work.

This fits with psychoanalytic theory, which acknowledges that hate is a developmentally important task. Green (2006) states that it is through the experience of hating that one can give up the expectation that the other person changes to fit with one's own needs. This enables acceptance of the other person as separate from us and where this fails, rage may ensue, this being a sign of unmet or frustrated dependence. This will be familiar to anyone who has cared for a hungry, tired baby or worked within in-patient mental health settings when the atmosphere is highly charged.

Conversely, hate facilitates differentiation; it delineates the sense of self, enabling acceptance of the other for who she or he is rather than who the practitioner needs them to be. This means being better able to make decisions about what would be most therapeutic (Green, 2006). This idea links with how important it is to know where the practitioner ends and the person in distress starts. Being merged with the other person risks overidentification, which in turn can lead to burnout and compassion fatigue, whilst extending this further, the consequences of not being able to acknowledge one's own feelings of hate and find a safe space to work through and process them impacts differentiation and acceptance of difference.

The importance of this when working with people who are experiencing disturbance is acknowledged by Ballatt, Campling and Maloney (2020, p. 53), who refer to the 'intrinsic horrors and anxieties' of the work. To return to the case example of David, at no point was there any curiosity about how unpopular he was with staff and patients. This denial of his impact did not get thought about in a therapeutic way; it was not contained. Yet denial does not mean this disturbance ceases to exist; it merely gets expressed in other ways, such as relief once the source of the irritation moves on, jokes at the others expense or scapegoating. In these circumstances, rather than being protective, this denial becomes damaging and even abusive unless there is time and space to reflect on and manage these difficult feelings.

Elton (2019, p. 313) wonders what reasons Winnicott would give, if he were alive, to explain why doctors hate their patients. As will be illustrated, this is not solely confined to medical staff and will be familiar to all who work in health and social care:

- 'Fear of making a significant mistake
- Time pressures; too many patients to see in too short a time
- Uncertainty about the diagnosis, or treatment plan
- Professional impotence when the patient's illness can't be cured
- Patients' unrealistic expectations about what modern medicine can achieve
- Patients challenging your professional knowledge
- Fear of being the subject of a complaint or a legal claim
- Exhaustion caused by working through the night
- Hunger and thirst through working a whole shift without a break
- Being on the receiving end of derogatory comments from patients
- Disgust at physical decay or deformity
- Fear of contagion
- Contempt at injuries caused by the patient's own behaviour
- Having to work in a part of the country where one is separated from family and friends
- Missing out on a special family celebration because one must work'

As Kahr (2014) comments in relation to Winnicott's paper, it serves as a stark reminder that even the most educated, experienced, and trained colleague can struggle in this work and that acknowledging hatred enables the practitioner to stay with the person in distress. As such, 'staying open to the needs and experience of the people one is trying to help in the face of one's own motivations and reactions to illness and social disturbance is essentially a psychological task' (Ballatt, Campling & Maloney, 2020, p. 55).

A psychological task needs psychological support, but where such a safe space to digest these feelings does not exist, hatred is likely to manifest in unthinking ways. This can be an example of acting out as defined earlier by Lemma (2016). An observable example is unnecessarily lengthy waits to have needs met in residential environments whilst staff attend to other tasks. Further examples include slamming a door when feelings of anger cannot be put into words, materialism to boost self-esteem and using substances to help numb emotions and memories.

In organisations, when the primary task(s) create anxiety, the anxiety may be linked to the fear of losing control of the rational self, and there is a risk of more irrational emotions taking over (Cardona, 2020). Whilst paradoxical, practitioners may need to split off part of their emotional experience to maintain their own mental health and to provide a reliable service (Cardona, 2020); in extreme examples, acting out may manifest in the damaging and abusive treatment of others.

A BBC Panorama documentary televised in 2022 starkly illustrated how undermined the psychological task to remain open to the needs of those using services in the face of one's own responses can be. It focused on an undercover report at The Edenfield Centre, a Regional Secure Unit in Greater Manchester Mental Health NHS Foundation Trust (GMMH) based in the UK. The primary task of this service is to offer a therapeutic, secure environment primarily for people who have mental health problems and an offending history. Working with people who present in disturbing states of mind coupled with an offending history means an intricate balance must be struck to meet this primary task which rests on providing practitioners with safe, containing support through effective leadership and a conducive organisational culture.

Following airing of the programme, NHS England commissioned an independent review of the Trust which was published in January 2024 (Shanley, 2024). The report does not shy away from using language to convey what it refers to as the 'horror' and 'appalling levels of abuse, humiliation and bullying of patients' (Shanley, 2024, p. i). It is commented upon that the Trust Board were more intent on focusing on expansion, reputation and meeting operational targets than high-quality care. Shanley (2024) comments on the levels of distress displayed by staff in GMMH and notes surprise at this. Overall, the report gives a flavour of the conditions patients and staff were subject to, paradoxically stating that attempts during the enquiry were made to engender a safe space to speak about their experience. This can only be concluded as the antithesis of the everyday experience of living and working at The Edenfield Centre. The report goes on to say that once the Panorama documentary aired, GMMH and NHS England took a number of actions including suspension of staff who were then dismissed from their employment; the chief executive officer resigned in June 2023, and at the time of writing, three ex-employees are subject to criminal investigation as reported in a local newspaper (Manchester Evening News).

From an ethical perspective, there is a clear rationale for removing staff from their contact with patients, but there is an associated loss with this. Shanley (2024) states that there was insufficient curiosity about the ongoing patient and staff experience across GMMH which contributed to missed opportunities for organisational learning across several services. With every decision, there is an associated loss, and in this instance, it may be reasonable to suggest that the insight and learning which could be gained from members of staff is lost as they leave. This represents the view that out of sight, out of mind helps remedy the underlying issues. This view is akin to the idea of a few bad apples, which is often used as a way of distancing the rest of the organisation from the behaviour of focus. Yet Freud (1914) conveyed that insight and awareness alone do not bring change. Fully interrogating the issues to harness crucial experiences and working through to process and resolve the underlying concerns is required if real change is to follow. Where there is commitment to real change in this way and opportunities to understand individual experiences, group dynamics and organisational culture are taken up. There is a chance to counter the point that there is

'a tendency to underestimate the effect of the group and a poor understanding of how group dynamics can influence behaviour. . . . We need to understand how kindness can be facilitated or undermined by the group dynamic' (Ballatt, Campling & Maloney, 2020, p. 67). Where kindness is fundamental to the primary task but is undermined by the group dynamic, it can be considered anti-task. Bion (1961) said that within a group, there is a desire to work on the primary task referred to as 'work-group mentality'. In contrast, the tendency to avoid work on the primary task, often driven by unconscious processes is referred to as 'basic assumption mentality'. The difference is that the former relies on facing reality, and the latter is an evasion of it when it is painful or anxiety provoking or causes conflict within the group.

In this context, anti-task can be seen to represent

a regressive pull in all of us which means benevolence slips into malevolence all too easily under the pressure of anxiety, perceived or real threats and, what I want to argue, is the lure of the 'gang', which promises a life without any of the pains that recognizing difference, dependency, the inevitability of death and vulnerability entails.

(Canham, 2002, p. 114)

This quote illustrates that under certain circumstances, we are all susceptible to the pull of the gang. Again, reflection on David's experience is pertinent and fits with the point made earlier that even the most educated, experienced and trained colleague can struggle in this work (Kahr, 2014). These processes are not confined to the disturbed but to the ordinary everyday experience of what it is to be a person in contact with other people.

The lure of the gang can be seen across society; for instance, as a member of the dominant group, diversity and difference are often attributed to 'the other' (Abrahams & Rohleder 2021). Under the circumstances described by Canham, (2002), those who are considered 'other' or 'different' by the majority, or not the majority but the dominant group, can become a target for the slip from benevolence to malevolence.

With reference to racism, Dalal (2006) suggests that the most common explanation for this is the mechanism of splitting, repression and projection. It is this mechanism that can enable the temptation to deny one's intolerable feelings and to locate them outside in others, a process which Morgan (2021) as a white, female psychoanalyst, refers to as 'white ignorance'. Yet Davids (2011) contends that internal racism belongs to the normal mind: 'some of us know our racism while others project it; either way, though, it is present in the mind. If at first, we cannot find it we probably have not looked hard enough' (p. 43). This can feel as controversial as Winnicott's ideas about hate in the countertransference, and Davids similarly urges engagement with rather than avoidance of the thoughts and feelings that are stirred up.

As a white therapist working with a black patient, Morgan (2021) states there are a variety of routes to take, firstly, to ignore it, but this is a denial of the uncomfortable feelings this difference may invoke for both; to acknowledge there is an issue but only one that exists for the black person; similarly this is a defence against the therapists own racist responses and therefore against shame and guilt. Finally is recognising there is a racist backdrop to society and as a white person, one cannot be free from that. This leads to acknowledgement that racism will affect the relationship and that a power differential exists which is above that between any patient and therapist. It is the management of this that Morgan (2021) states can lead to the point when the issue is not an issue. The point here is extended to practitioners and people in receipt of health and social care.

Taking Morgan's (2021) points, it would be remiss not to retrospectively think about racism in the case example of David. He was not the only minoritised black man on the unit during his admission, but this was coupled with the illegality of David's right to stay in the country. Thorough consideration of the impact that intersectionality has in assisting, understanding and resisting repeating damaging dynamics are key here.

It is reasonable to suggest that there is a need in contemporary health and social care to take up the psychodynamic position that facing one's fears can paradoxically make a situation safer. By being open to the most feared impulses, thoughts and feelings, they can be contained in the mind, reducing their ability to produce anxiety and enabling the problem to be faced (Davids, 2011).

Having stressed the importance of psychotherapeutic approaches in enabling an understanding of prejudice and enabling the toleration of hate in safe ways, it should be acknowledged that psychoanalytic theory and its application are not beyond reproach. Chamberlain (2022) draws attention to Freud's neglect of women in the development of psychoanalytic theory. Similarly, given mental health's questionable history with sexualities beyond the heteronormative perspective, it is perhaps unsurprising that the British Psychoanalytic Council (BPC), as one of the regulatory bodies for psychoanalysis and psychotherapy felt compelled to offer this position as follows, but what might be more perplexing is that this statement was not issued until 2011: '[T]he BPC does not accept that a homosexual orientation is evidence of disturbance of the mind or development' (2021).

It is fair to suggest that even accounting for the view that 'psychoanalytic theory that underpins psychodynamic psychotherapy is the richest and most sophisticated set of ideas concerning the functioning of the human mind that we currently have available to us' (Peter Fonagy in Abrahams & Rohleder, 2021), it is not above criticism in terms of prejudice and discrimination. This demonstrates the point being made in this chapter that safe spaces are required to acknowledge, work through and process the inevitable prejudices we all hold as health and social care practitioners. In doing, transparency may be enabled regarding 'the infinities of differences (and similarities) between two human beings, how and why are we led in a particular moment to experience and construe one difference as primary and to render the others less meaningful?' (Dalal, 2006, p. 151). It is in taking up such a position that we might face our own limitations and try to guard against hatred in the work.

Implications and recommendations

The following section in this chapter develops key points from the discussion to consider their implications and to make recommendations for health and social care. The starting point for this is to stress that neglecting to consider the manifestations of hatred within the context of care is a risk not worth taking.

Being open to hatred

The difficulties in doing this where a safe supportive space is non-existent have been discussed along with the impact of this on the primary task. In an attempt to address this, there is a need to provide containing, thoughtful support where difficulties can be safely broached. Ideally this would begin in programmes of study leading to professional registration, where knowledge, skills and attitudes are being formed during the preparation of health and social care practitioners. However, this is not standard practice: 'the human capacity for treating others cruelly has much preoccupied thinkers . . . but hardly gets a mention in professional curricula' (Ballatt, Campling & Maloney, 2020, p. 67).

The relationships forged between students and academics mean there is an opportunity to offer support to enable curiosity. As such, professional programmes leading to qualification in the health and social care professions are an ideal opportunity to support students in this context; as Ballatt, Campling, and Maloney (2020) state, 'It is important to be curious about oneself, to recognise the shadow side to the declared motivation for choosing the job that one does, and to be aware of resonances between the work and one's own life experiences' (p. 53).

It is reasonable to suggest that lacking curiosity in this way and the impact of functioning in a closed culture (Shanley, 2024) contributed to the abusive behaviour of staff towards patients reported in the independent review of GMMH NHS Foundation Trust. One strategy in trying to address this is the use of external supervisors who are not only skilled at identifying group dynamics and understand conscious and unconscious processes within an organisational culture but also can support practitioners in working through these impactful experiences.

Skilled supervision

Evans (2021) states that staff function effectively when they can empathise with the service user's situation without becoming overwhelmed or overidentified. This comes from reflection, clinical discussion and supervision to provide a psychological space for thinking.

This cannot be achieved in isolation; it requires the input of another to help identify blind spots in a constructive way that refrains from shaming the person and possibly leading to further denial that an issue exists. It is here that there needs to be a frame for sharing experiences, working through them and in doing, processing the more difficult and troubling aspects. As stated, it is

> important to give greater management attention to care for the carers, and how containment of anxiety is in danger of becoming a neglected management function . . . non managerial supervision, reflective practice, even an in-house counselling service might be seen both as a necessary resource to stressed staff and a way for the system to be self-reflective.
>
> (Dartington, 2017, p. 169)

In this respect, reflective practice (Yiu et al., 2025) and work discussion (Youell, 2024) groups have shown benefits. This format has utility across all areas of health and social care, and whilst it is important to have a psychoanalytically trained facilitator to support the frame, you do not have to be trained in psychoanalysis to make effective use of such a space (Foster, 2020).

Embracing difference

The case example and previous discussion have highlighted the importance of appreciating intersectionality in relation to people who use and deliver health and social care. It is also important to acknowledge that some practitioners may feel anxious, consciously and unconsciously, about working with differences (Abrahams & Rohleder, 2021). However, as Abrahams and Rohleder (2021) go on to state, it is important to recognise that differences exist between people; the service user and practitioner have different identities. Holding in mind the conscious thought to consider 'Who are you?' (Belkin, 2020) and embracing rather than avoiding difficult conversations links to the idea of psychological safety.

This needs to be both internally experienced and externally supported to enable practitioners to feel psychologically present and safe. The consequences of an absence of psychological safety were detailed in the findings from the independent review of GMMH NHS Foundation Trust (Shanley, 2024). This requires good leadership and is a point that Canham (2002) makes in relation to the difference between working as a group and functioning as a gang: 'I think the presence of figures in authority who can maintain a thoughtful and considerate attitude towards all those for whom they have responsibility inclines people towards grouping rather than ganging' (Canham, 2002, p. 125).

Being psychologically present is key to the functioning, development and stability of staff (Cardona, 2020). It is under such conditions that difference and identities can be thoughtfully explored: 'a well-functioning group or an individual in this state of mind can tolerate, explore and value difference, alternative viewpoints and the tensions and potential for creativity these throw up' (Canham, 2002, p. 113).

Such supportive spaces enable a focus on the emotional impact of the work, and whilst bearing in mind the preparation required to use countertransference as a way of understanding the inner world of another, our countertransference is a useful early warning system (Abrahams & Rohleder, 2021). In this context, attentive reflection and curiosity can enable all practitioners, trained in psychodynamic approaches or not, to be informed by this in a helpful way and is a view endorsed by Obholzer:

> In order to manage one's personal and organizational life, one needs to have an understanding of the processes that manifest themselves in all areas of one's life. The key is the realization that one's picture of the world and its functioning is solely one's own . . . one has on a daily basis, to monitor not only one's own assumptions but also make allowances for the fact that any work or social intercourse requires an acknowledgement of the other perspectives.
>
> (p. 139)

Conclusion

In this chapter, I applied Winnicott's (1949) paper 'Hate in the Countertransference' to contemporary health and social care. I proposed the need for safe places to support practitioners in managing the difficult thoughts and feelings such as hate that can arise from close connection with the experiences of people who use services.

In the chapter, I urged the need for a containing, psychologically safe, holding environment to help prevent unwanted aspects of the dynamic between practitioner and individual using the service. Examples have illustrated the negative impact on the primary task where this has not been provided and is countered with suggestions as to how high-quality health and social care, which is effective and acceptable to those in receipt of it, can be supported even in the challenging contemporary context of health and social care.

References

Abrahams, D., & Rohleder, P. (2021) *A Clinical Guide to Psychodynamic Psychotherapy*. London & New York. Routledge Taylor & Francis Group.

Ballatt, J., Campling, P., & Maloney, C. (2020) *Intelligent Kindness; Rehabilitating the Welfare State*. 2nd Edition. Cambridge. Cambridge University Press.

Belkin, M. (2020) Who is queer around here? Overcoming rigid thinking and relating in patient and analyst in Belkin, M., & White, C. (eds) *Intersectionality and Relational Psychoanalysis*. London & New York. Routledge Taylor & Francis Group.

Bion, W.R. (1961) *Experiences in Groups and Other Papers*. London. Tavistock.

Bott Spillius, E., Milton, J., Garvey, P., Couve, C., & Steiner, D. (2011) *The New Dictionary of Kleinian Thought.* London & New York. Routledge Taylor & Francis Group.

BPC. (2021) PPNow 2021 homosexuality statement of regret – British Psychoanalytic Council (bpc.org.uk) Accessed 29th April 2025.

Canham, H. (2002) Group and gang states of mind, *Journal of Child Psychotherapy*, 28:2, 113–127, https://doi.org/10.1080/00754170210143753

Cardona, F. (2020) *Work Matters. Consulting to Leaders and Organizations in the Tavistock Tradition*. London & New York. Routledge Taylor & Francis group.

Chamberlain, M. (2022) *Misogyny in Psychoanalysis*. Oxfordshire. Phoenix Publishing House.

Dalal, F. (2006) Racism: Processes of detachment, dehumanization, and hatred, *The Psychoanalytic Quarterly*, LXXV, 131–161.

Dartington, T. (2017) The organisational context for good care in Vaspe, A. (ed.) *Psychoanalysis, the NHS, and Mental Health Work Today.* London. Karnac.

Davids, F. (2011) *Internal Racism: A Psychoanalytic Approach to Race and Difference*. Basingstoke. Palgrave Macmillan.

Elton, C. (2019) *Also Human the Inner Lives of Doctors*. London. Windmill Books.

Evans, M. (2021) *Psychoanalytic Thinking in Mental Health Settings*. London & New York. Routledge Taylor & Francis Group.

Fonagy, P. (2021) Forward in Abrahams, D., & Rohleder, P. (eds) *A Clinical Guide to Psychodynamic Psychotherapy*. London & New York. Routledge Taylor & Francis Group.

Foster, C. (2020) Investigating the impact of a psychoanalytic nursing development group within an adolescent psychiatric intensive care unit (PICU), *Archives of Psychiatric Nursing*, 34:6, 481–491.

Freud, S. (1914) Remembering, repeating and working through (further recommendations on the technique of psycho-analysis II) in *The Standard Edition of the Complete Psychological Works of Sigmund Freud*, Vol. 12, 145–156. Hogarth Press and The Institute of Psychoanalysis.

Gabbard, G.O. (1994) Classic article. *Journal of Psychotherapy Practice and Research,* 3:4, Fall.

Green, L.B. (2006) The value of hate in the countertransference, *Clinical Social Work Journal*, 34:2, 187–199.

Kahr, B. (2014) *The Winnicott Tradition: Lines of Development-Evolution of Theory and Practice over the Decades*. M.B. Spelman & F. Thomson-Salo (ed.). Taylor & Francis Group.

Lemma, A. (2016) *Introduction to the Practice of Psychoanalytic Psychotherapy*. John Wiley & Sons.

Manchester Evening News. https://www.manchestereveningnews.co.uk/news/greater-manchester-news/police-send-file-crown-lawyers-30527966 accessed 29th April 2025.

Morgan, H. (2021) *The Work of Whiteness a Psychoanalytic Perspective.* London & New York. Routledge Taylor & Francis Group.

Obholzer, A. (2021) *Workplace Intelligence Unconscious Forces and How to Manage Them.* London & New York. Routledge Taylor & Francis group.

Rice, A.K. (1963) *The Enterprise and its Environment.* London. Tavistock Publications.

Shanley, O. (2024) Independent Review of Greater Manchester Mental Health NHS Foundation Trust Final Report, January 2024. https://www.england.nhs.uk/north-west/wp-content/uploads/sites/48/2024/01/Final-Report-Independent-Review-of-GMMH-January-2024.pdf accessed 29th April 2025.

Winnicott, D.W. (1949) Hate in the counter-transference. *The International Journal of Psycho-Analysis*, 30, 69–74.

Yiu, P.L.J., McDonogh, A., Gill, H., & Billings, J. (2025) Creating a culture, not just a space – a qualitative investigation into reflective practice groups in inpatient mental health settings from the perspectives of facilitators and attendees, *PLoS ONE*, 20:1, e0316030, https://doi.org/10.1371/journal.pone.0316030.

Youell, B. (2024) Introducing psychoanalytic observation through work discussion: The relationship between experiential learning and theory, *Infant Observation*, 27:2, 130–138, https://doi.org/10.1080/13698036.2024.2443883.

Chapter 4

To be or not to be detached or emotionally involved – that is the question of Heimann's 'On Counter-Transference' (1950)

Suryia Nayak and Alasdair Forrest

Introduction

In the 2020 Royal College of Nursing (RCN) Bulletin on the theme of emotionally demanding, an agency nurse is quoted saying, 'I don't need to work hard to feel for people in my care, but I do work hard to leave my own needs and feelings at the door and pick them up again on the way out' (McIlroy, 2020). Here the nurse is telling us how she manages the emotional labour of her role, where feeling for the patient is not the hard task. The nurse tells us that the hard task is identifying and separating out feelings that belong to her from feelings that belong to the people in her care. The nurse goes a step further to tell us that she picks up her own feelings, emotions and needs that belong to her after she leaves the patient 'on her way out'.

The questions that this chapter grapples with are How do we know what feelings belong to who in our work with patients/people we work with? Is there a clear distinction between the feelings of the practitioner and the feelings of the people who seek health and social care services? What would happen if our feelings and our bodily sensations as practitioners were not left at the door? What does 'pick them up again on the way out' mean? How might we make use of the feelings and embodied responses that we experience during and after contact/encounters with people who need health and social care? "'Too involved' or 'unable to cope': how can we bring emotions into social work?" (Gilbey, 2017) on the one hand speaks to the fear of recriminations and/or a lack of professional boundaries whilst on the other hand asking 'How can we bring emotions into social work?', which is a curious question for a relationship-based profession where being emotionally attuned and coproduction are key characteristics and values.

How do we understand these actions of a therapist's behaviour/reaction in the situation where her patient, repeatedly and for months, arrives late for their therapy session? On the occasion when the patient arrives on time, the therapist cannot remember the code to the door into the therapy room – a code that the therapist has used for years and has never forgotten. The consequence was that the therapy session started late due to the therapist not being able to remember the code. Could it be that the therapist was unconsciously enacting her feelings of anger, frustration and powerlessness that had built up over the months of tolerating her patient's

DOI: 10.4324/9781003541660-5

lateness, that she thought she had worked hard to leave her own needs and feelings at the door until the session had ended? Could it be that the therapist unconsciously made them late as pay back for all the times she had to wait in limbo not knowing if the patient would turn up? Should this therapist take time out? Is she too emotionally involved? Can she cope?

These contemporary questions and issues are not new. For decades, psychodynamic and psychoanalytic therapists have argued over the meaning and application of the word 'countertransference', which is about the emotional and bodily reactions in the therapist from being with their patient. In 1950, Paula Heimann wrote a paper called 'On Counter-Transference' which opens with the statement, 'Many [practitioners] are afraid and feel guilty when they become aware of feelings towards their patients and consequently aim at avoiding any emotional response and at becoming completely unfeeling and "detached"'. Heimann provides a way of thinking about and experiencing emotions that are invoked by being in close proximity to uncomfortable, often unbearable, conditions of vulnerability and distress experienced by the people, families and communities that constitute caseloads seeking relief and repair. Rather than viewing 'counter-transference is nothing but a source of trouble' (Heimann, 1950, p. 81), Heimann offers a language and a model that sees the emotional dynamics between practitioner and persons seeking support as an invaluable source of information and resource for understanding symptomology and constructing formulation, assessments and intervention or care plans/treatment. Indeed, it could be argued that countertransference is the equivalent of living case notes. The contemporary relevance of Heimann's ideas from the 1950s is brought to life through our case example, followed by an overview of Heimann's key messages 'on counter-transference' which we link together in our discussion and conclusion.

Countertransference has had a shifting definition and reception since Freud (1910) first mentioned the idea, saying the analyst had to recognise countertransference in themselves and *bewältigen* ('manage', 'struggle against', 'combat') this idea (*daß der Arzt diese Gegenübertragung in sich erkennen und bewältigen müsse*). *Bewältigen* derives ultimately from the word for violence (DWDS, 2025). In other words, the view was that countertransference was an obstacle to the therapeutic process.

The tendency has since been either to see countertransference as being of significant importance or a barrier to analytic work, often by speaking about slightly different ideas of what the countertransference is. Is countertransference the sum of all the feelings a clinician has in relation to their patient? Or should there be an attempt to restrict countertransference solely to the part of the feelings of the clinician that do not belong to them and solely relate these feelings to something generated by the patient? Is countertransference always liable to distort the thinking of the clinician or can it give them important information? How might countertransference be connected to the social context that the patient inhabits? Can countertransference enable understanding of power, privilege and position when relating across intersectional differences between patient and practitioner?Heimann's work 'On

Counter-Transference' sees countertransference as a creation of the patient in the mind of the analyst which can be understood by the analyst, and this understanding used as an important aspect of the treatment.

Case example

Nadja was referred by her general practitioner for talking therapy following extensive investigations into the cause of her symptoms of debilitating exhaustion and decreasing capacity to hear. Investigations with a consultant audiologist and specialist in myalgic encephalomyelitis/chronic fatigue syndrome showed no impairment in the mechanics of her ear and nothing to indicate a biological cause for her chronic tiredness.

During the therapy sessions, Nadja frequently asks for the therapist to repeat his sentences, to speak louder and to use gestures to communicate. The therapist usually grants these requests, slowing down, emphasising words, talking louder and using an improvised form of sign language but is wondering if this is the right way to proceed. He notices that Nadja's requests happen when they are edging close to a feeling that is directly linked to Nadja's childhood, particularly her relationship to her mum. He is becoming increasingly tired of feeling stuck, that the therapy is not progressing, that each session feels like Groundhog Day.

The therapist is beginning to physically (nausea, headaches, tiredness, sleepiness) and emotionally dread the sessions but feels torn between not wanting to be anywhere near Nadja and trying, as a white male, to be inclusive of Nadja's identified intersectional characteristics of being a Pakistani Muslim woman with a self-declared hearing impairment. The therapist is finding it hard to know whether he is unwell himself and needs to get the nausea, headaches and tiredness checked out or if he is burnt out and needs to take a break from the vicarious trauma or perhaps there is something about Nadja that is getting inside him. The therapist feels guilty, shamed and powerless by these thoughts and feelings which have prevented him from bringing the situation to supervision.

Overview of the paper

Countertransference is unconscious communication

Paula Heimann's 'On Counter-Transference' (1950) builds on the foundational idea that people communicate their thoughts, experiences and feelings unconsciously. Heimann declares,

> I believe that with more thorough investigation of counter-transference . . . we may come to work out more fully the way in which the character of the counter-transference corresponds to the nature of the patient's unconscious impulses and defences operative at the actual time.
>
> (1950, p. 84)

Countertransference is unconscious communication. Heimann works on the premise that

> the analyst's unconscious understands that of his patient. This rapport on the deep level comes to the surface in the form of feelings which the analyst notices in response to his patient, in his 'counter-transference'. This is the most dynamic way in which his patient's voice reaches him.
>
> (1950, p. 82)

Indeed, the key argument of 'On Counter-Transference' is that the practitioner's conscious cognitive abilities to discern the experience, meaning and root of the patient/client's situation can never be as attuned as, or lags behind, the practitioner's unconscious reactions to the experience, meaning and root of the patient/client's situation. Heimann explains that the practitioner's

> immediate emotional response to his patient is a significant pointer to the patient's unconscious processes and guides him towards fuller understanding [] often the emotions roused in him are much nearer to the heart of the matter than his reasoning, or, to put it in other words, his unconscious perception of the patient's unconscious is more acute and in advance of his conscious conception of the situation.
>
> (1950, p. 82)

The starting point for understanding the importance of countertransference is that it is a communication from the unconscious, transmitted unconsciously, and it provides insight into what is held in the unconscious. What usually determines whether something is held in the realm of the conscious (known) or held in the realm of the unconscious (unknown) is the degree to which a thought, experience and feeling can be tolerated. The more unbearable the thing, the more likely it is to be in the realm of the unconscious, highly defended to keep it unknown, unspoken, unfelt, unthought about, patrolled by unconscious defences that often cause as much distress, destruction and disturbance as what is unbearable.

For example, the unbearable experience of a cruelly critical and/or emotional unavailable parent may be held in the unconscious, managed by defence mechanisms that ward off the tsunami of affect associated with the experience. A key strategy that the unconscious uses to defend against intolerable, disturbing feelings is to relocate and identify the disturbance elsewhere. Examples of relocation strategies include projection and transference. Relocation is as if the disturbance/bad bits are in another person – split off to a different time, place, setting, group or person and to unconsciously clinch the deal, the place/space of the relocated disturbance becomes equated/identified as disturbed/disturbance. Here, the relocation of that which is unbearable is achieved through projection and identification, known as projective identification, of the unwanted bad bits on to another; It is also achieved through transference of past relationships/attachment experiences onto the present relationships/attachments. Countertransference is the unconscious communication arising out of projective identification and transference.

The idea of transference is that patients transfer past experiences to the present (Freud, 1912). This is the sense that human beings develop a template of what relationships will be like as they grow into adulthood from formative experiences in childhood. This is the template through which the patient has learned to organise relationships in general, or of a particular type, can be seen in their relationship to the therapist and/or health and social care practitioners. Broadening out the application of this idea, it is also possible to see how intergenerational transmission of the past into the present could be a type of collective social unconscious transference. The interpersonal and the collective social unconscious levels of transference are mutually constitutive.

The process that leads to the development of the countertransference is projective identification. This is a process where the patient unconsciously disclaims an aspect of themselves and relocates it in the therapist and/or health and social care practitioner: for example, 'projective identification may permit a patient to localize aggression outside the self' (Kernberg, 1987, p. 797). Such is the unconscious force of projective identification that the therapist and/or health and social care practitioner themselves may begin to act, think or identify with what has been projected. The task for the practitioner, and here is where countertransference is useful, is to contain the projection, recognise it as arising from the patient, and help them understand the aspect of themselves they project, in time, and with care (Kernberg, 1965; Ogden, 1979).

As with transference, it is possible to see how the process of projective identification can apply more broadly within society, within the collective social unconscious. Here, groups, neighbourhoods, nations, historical periods/events and institutions can be locators or locations of projective identification. The social construction of intersectional racism is a prime example of locating that which is deemed to be 'bad' into people from the Global South who have black and brown skins.

'Counter' implies additional factors

As is often the case with analytic terms, the plain reading of the word can be a source of confusion. For example, the prefix 'counter' in the word countertransference is not to be misunderstood in the literal meaning of the word 'counter' which we could assume refers to being antithetical or in opposition, offsetting, hindering, moving in the opposite direction. Samuel Stein called countertransference an 'ill-chosen term' because 'analyst took it literally to mean the analyst's transference as opposed to the patient's transference – exactly the opposite of what Paula Heimann intended' (1991, p. 235).

The radical work on the countertransference in Heimann's writing is to suggest that the countertransferential feelings in the therapist are essentially creations of the patient: the therapist is drawn into enacting something that originated in the internal world of the patient (Gabbard, 2001). Indeed, Heimann's work enables us to go a step further to think about countertransference as a co-creation between patient and therapist, and in this regard, she was way ahead of contemporary discourses on relational co-creation approaches. Heimann states,

> it is a *relationship* between two persons. What distinguishes this relationship from others, is not the presence of feelings in one partner, the patient, and their absence in the other, the analyst, but above all the degree of the feelings experienced and the use made of them, these factors being interdependent.
>
> (1950, p. 81, emphasis in original)

The key here is the interdependency of feeling (between patient and practitioner) and how the practitioner makes use of the feelings as insight.

On the subject of the prefix 'counter', Heimann wrote,

> I am using the term 'counter-transference' to cover all the feelings which the analyst experiences towards his patient. It may be argued that this use of the term is not correct, and that counter-transference simply means transference on the part of the analyst. However, I would suggest that the prefix 'counter' implies additional factors.
>
> (1950, p. 81)

These additional factors include using 'all the feelings' that the practitioner experiences towards the patient/clients' as important information into the root of the patient/clients' mental distress that is safely tucked away in the unconscious, hidden and not consciously revealed.

The additional factors that the prefix 'counter' could include are the practitioner's physical embodied responses towards their patient/client. Common examples of somatic countertransference include 'headaches, nausea, aches, pains, sleepiness, sexual arousal, dizziness and trembling felt by the psychotherapist in session' (Margarian, 2014, p. 137). The additional factors or insights into the patient/client's unconscious that somatic countertransference gives to the practitioner is an important reminder that the experiences of mental distress and trauma do not comply with the Cartesian dualism whereby mind and body are conceived as separate (ibid). The imperative to attend to somatic countertransference is amplified with the growing demographics of racial diversity, including migrants, asylum seekers and refugees in need of health and social care support, patients/clients whose trauma is shaped by living in the social context of racialized misogyny. Being attuned to somatic countertransference can assist practitioners in appreciating that 'theatres of the body are intersectional' (Nayak, 2021, p. 524).

Countertransference: a practitioner's tool

Heimann states, 'My thesis is that the analyst's emotional response to his patient within the analytic situation represents one of the most important tools for his work. The analyst's counter-transference is an instrument of research into the patient's unconscious' (1950, p. 81). The key phrases here are 'emotional response' and 'patient's unconscious' and the way that Heinmann tells us that the practitioner's emotional relating to the patient is a gateway into the patient's unknown inner psychological world. Countertransference gives insight into that which the patient would otherwise be unable to consciously tell or know. Heimann tells us that countertransference is 'one of the most important tools'; it could be argued that Heimann is pointing health and social care practitioners to the potential of countertransference to help inform 'a more sensitive diagnostic process, generate accurate and clinically meaningful case formulations, and facilitate planning effective therapeutic interventions' (Tanzilli et al., 2022, p. 51).

Evenly hovering attention

The importance of active listening is stressed in all health and social care disciplines and correlated with improved patient outcomes in nursing, repeatedly highlighted in Serious Case Review recommendations and seen as the cornerstone of effective care. Active listening in psychoanalytic terms could be framed in Heimann's terms as the need for 'an evenly hovering attention in order to follow the patient's free associations, and that this enables him to listen simultaneously on many levels' (1950, p. 82).

Heimann's use of the words 'evenly' and 'hovering' assists the practitioner in two significant ways. Hovering attention or hovering listening and feeling enables the practitioner 'to perceive the manifest and the latent meaning of his patient's words, the allusions and implications, the hints to former sessions, the references to childhood situations behind the description of current relationships' (Heimann, 1950, p. 82). Evenly or equally spread attention helps the practitioner to avoid 'the danger of becoming preoccupied with any one theme and remains receptive for the significance of changes in themes and of the sequences and gaps in the patient's associations' (ibid). Heimann's ideas about 'an evenly hovering attention' include that 'the analyst's emotional sensitivity needs to be extensive rather than intensive, differentiating and mobile' (ibid). The point is not to be too intensely fixated on one feeling/theme, which is quite a task for the practitioner, who may be overwhelmed with 'violent emotions of any kind, of love or hate, helpfulness or anger' (ibid).

Work on yourself: supervision/reflection

Heimann is clear that the task of therapeutic work is not 'mechanical' or simply a 'purely intellectual procedure'; the task for the practitioner is to emotionally sustain and contain the countertransference feeling and somatic reactions stirred up 'as opposed to discharging them (which is what the patient does) in order to subordinate them to the analytic task in which he functions as the patient's mirror reflection' (1950, p. 82). Resisting the impulse to act on and/or discharge feelings put into the practitioner by the patient/client through projective identification is an arduous task. Heimann states, 'I do not consider it right for the analyst [and mental health practitioner] to communicate his feelings to his patient. In my view such honesty is more in the nature of a confession and a burden to the patient' (1950, p. 83). The practitioner needs support including spaces where they can unpack and be helped to be curious about their countertransference. Such is the force of countertransference that it often stops the capacity to think, especially in the here and now of the therapeutic session.

Heimann cautions that 'counter-transference . . . is not without danger. It does not represent a screen for the analyst's shortcomings' (1950, p. 83). The disturbance of overwhelming affect and embodied experiences of holding the patient/client's split off bad and mad parts, as hard as it is for the practitioner to sustain, is not an excuse for shortcomings such as breaking boundaries. The fact that countertransference is unconscious makes it difficult for the practitioner to decipher or make conscious. However, 'unexamined countertransference can interfere with effective treatment. For this reason, self-reflection on the part of psychiatrists [and mental health practitioner] is essential' (Vogel, 2024, p. 183). The problem with self-reflection on its own is that the duration and weight of the countertransference usually requires the help of supervision and at times the need for the practitioner to undergo their own therapy to work out how and why the experience of being with the patient/client is so triggering. Heimann advises that the practitioner undertake their own analysis to work through their own 'infantile conflicts and anxieties paranoid and depressive), so that he can easily establish contact with his own unconscious [in order not to] impute to his patient what belongs to himself' (1950, p. 83).

Whilst Heimann does not directly address how and why countertransference exists within and is shaped by social constructions of subjectivity/identity, it is incumbent on all health and social care practitioners to rigorously unpack the ways in which the dynamics of power, privilege and position operate unconsciously in the relationship with patients/clients; this entails staying with discomfort. For example, drawing on Fanon's work, Oliver (2001, p. 34) argues that 'racist social structures create racist psychic structures'. If this is the case, then the form, movement and manifestation of countertransference cannot be divorced from the social contexts of both patient/client and practitioner. Indeed, back in 1951, just a year after Heimann's paper was published, Viola Bernard presented her ideas on cultural factors in psychoanalytic treatment at the Annual Meeting of American Psychoanalytic Association. Bernard stated, 'often the unconscious foundations and psychodynamics of prejudice have not been worked with and worked through in the analyst's own analysis (Bernard, 1953, p. 258).

Discussion

We return to the case example, now with Heimann's ideas about a more expansive view of countertransference. The therapist is trying to understand something about Nadja's inner world to help her understand it about herself. He has been confronted with a hard-to-manage, diffuse set of physical symptoms that seem, under the lens of countertransference, quite obviously linked to his contact with Nadja but are not experienced in abstract terms at all: they are experienced as very much in him. His experience of the difficulty with her hearing is an additional dimension, and he wished really not to hear things, or have them heard, in supervision.

When he did recognise that he had to take Nadja to supervision and confront these issues, he was surprised to find the supervisor's mind more alive than his. She was not so bound up with this emotional and physical experience and had room to think and promote thinking. She asked him to think about tiredness, wakefulness and sleep in Nadja's early life – what did he recall about that? He suddenly felt ashamed as he remembered that Nadja had hardly slept as a child at all with a father who was always returning late, drunk and perpetrating domestic violence; she could not have rest. Instead, she learned to be alert always – and was permanently tired as a child as a result. He could start to feel more alert to her experience as they thought more.

In supervision, they thought about what could have been put in the therapist's bodily experience as the only way to communicate this upsetting, frustrating and disabling affect that was such a part of Nadja's awareness. Heimann's sense of the countertransference is that something has gradually been created in the therapist. An intrapersonal drama in the patient turned into an interpersonal drama, and that turned into an intrapersonal drama in the therapist. It held all the potential to be turned again into an interpersonal drama between them as he was on the threshold of acting based on the countertransferential feelings.

It could be that Nadja is essentially conflicted about getting close to feelings as they are associated with danger: anyone who was noticed in her house was at risk of violence, and she had long ago determined not to be noticed. The affect that underlies this wariness could be anger at the feeling of dependence it arouses, or terror at that feeling, or frustration at an inability to be noticed; to start thinking in supervision, the therapist and his supervisor started to take that as a hypothesis.

The constant communication difficulties generate annoyance in the therapist, who is not necessarily completely aware of the depth of his feeling. When he feels impotent, unable to proceed and also physically spent, he is given an emotional experience on behalf of the patient. More able to understand this as countertransference, in supervision he can start to think more about the patient's symptom, and this becomes a focus of his listening. He discovers that Nadja only stopped hearing so well when she left home as an adult and was no longer responsible for listening out for danger towards her siblings. By doing the difficult work of containing this, he is able to take on an emotional experience that changes his understanding of the patient and can change the way he listens to her. This opens up the possibility of responding to her symptoms with an interpretation that at the right time may help her understand why she has taken on these ways of living. The therapist's own attunement may be different depending on their nature: they may feel at home with a language of the body, which this therapist's experience with the patient is having tested in him. Or, they may be more attuned to emotional experience, or patterns of behaviour, or cognitions, or impulses to act.

Freud wrote about how symptoms, or dream images, were over-determined: they could at any moment mean many things crystallised in one thing. That is the difficulty of analytic work and also the source of some criticism of it. The important message from Heimann's work, though, is that the affect experienced by the patient and communicated may not be truly perceived unless the therapist allows themselves to be bent out of shape by the patient's projective processes. Here, the therapist was bent out of shape and feeling unexpected things, and that gave him access to an emotionally engaged process of trying to understand his patient that surpassed the potential of his attempts to access the meaning of the symptom cognitively. This is not for that reason, though, a licence to act and not think. Heimann argues the opposite, whilst recognising that being bent out of shape in this way is inevitable. It took supervision and careful thought to recognise what was a counter-transferential experience: the countertransference does not emerge carrying a sign saying it is a creation of the patient; it feels a part of the therapist.

This example in the setting of individual psychotherapy makes the situation clear, but its application is far broader. Here, there is a somatic aspect to the countertransference, but what if the countertransferential experience is more clearly linked to emotion? In this example, a professional notices something about an emotion evoked in him that he can link to the experience of the patient.

Vignette

A housing officer calls his senior colleague for help. He says that he has been helping his client, who is a woman with a recent history of being the victim of domestic violence, to find a new permanent tenancy and move out of the women's shelter. He has offered her several tenancies, but whilst seeming quite placid when viewing them, she has turned them down for seemingly spurious reasons. He felt a strong urge to tell her he was placing her in a notorious high-rise apartment block but stopped himself, recognising this was unreasonable.

In their discussion, the senior housing officer might help their colleague think about what the client might be doing here. The client, who looks calm outwardly, may well be preoccupied with some ambivalence about moving on from the women's shelter. The underlying affect may well be fear, or it could be a more complex mix of feelings. Is she so frightened of going back into a permanent tenancy because of her experience of violence that a process is set up where she is inducing the housing officer to do something that would make her frightened: placing her in a high-rise flat that is notorious in the local area? Here, the housing officer has recognised that he is about to do something that is alien to him, and without necessarily recognising the reason for it, seeks help by discussing it with a colleague so he can understand it rather than just act. In the discussion, he can work out that he is annoyed with the patient and feeling he cannot live up to her standards, which replicates some of how she felt in the abusive relationship. The therapist working with Nadja, though, also has an emotional aspect to the countertransference: the dread, guilt and shame. These aspects of the countertransference are almost suffocated by the feelings of tiredness and sickness that are so somatically present but are there, nonetheless.

The countertransferential experience may be more in the realm of cognition and impulse to action, with the emotional experience of the patient communicated less directly.

Vignette

An elderly psychiatrist sees in her outpatient clinic a depressed patient who really is not getting better. The patient, a woman in her late 70s, speaks frequently of her children, who live abroad, but the psychiatrist has not found herself paying much attention to this. She starts an appointment thinking of admitting the patient to hospital for electroconvulsive therapy, but as the patient talks more, she has a strong impulse to tell the patient she could not be helped and to discharge her. She suddenly blushes.

Here, the psychiatrist has strong impulses at almost the same time both to provide the maximum amount of containment she could to the patient – admitting her to hospital – and to completely estrange herself from her. Recognising this impulse, she feels a sense of shame. Here, she could be responding to the patient's conflicting feelings about her children abroad: perhaps a pride in how they have managed to get on in life but also an annoyance that they are not near and seem to ignore her and a sense of humiliation that she would now be dependent on them. The psychiatrist is put in a position of being like the daughter of the patient – having both a (perhaps guilty) impulse to look after her and a wish she would just go away. She gets the sense of the underlying shameful affect by her blush.

In the situation of supervised individual therapy, where the therapist is not a blank screen by any means but provides a regular, consistent frame to the treatment, there are fewer moving parts, and that means that it can be easier to perceive these phenomena. As the number of moving parts increases – and as the frame slackens – the difficulty increases. To take the example of the kind of communication that comes through the countertransferential experience of fatigue and dread from Nadja's case, it is impossible for the clinician to have access to this if they are in a situation where the system simply allows them to avoid contact with the patient, where it may well be expected that someone else would cover at short notice in a large team or where caseload allocations change rapidly in an organisation.

Equally, if supervision were inadequate and had more of a case-management style or there were a strong impulse towards shorter treatments, the patient could be seen as not progressing or not suitable by a busy supervisor, foreclosing the prospect of the therapist being able to be bent out of shape by these projective processes and think about them. He could respond defensively to his difficulty in saying to himself he could not understand someone with an intersectional identity like Nadja and that she would be suitable for a form of therapy more focused on a different cultural understanding of illness or specific to those who are deaf. This pressure to discharge countertransferential feelings in a neglectful or abusive way, excluding the patient's experience and denying their needs, is a risk if the capacities of the professionals to contain projections are overwhelmed. For example, there is a significant difference between the responses of the elderly psychiatrist and of Nadja's therapist, as well as the response in this next vignette.

Vignette

A woman who had repeatedly gone to the police saying she was pregnant following sexual assaults, when it was clear to all involved that this repeated presentation over years was not about recent sexual assault, was referred by her general practitioner to a psychiatric service. When she told the psychiatrist she was pregnant, she was discharged and referred to a perinatal mental health service, where an ultrasound showed she was not pregnant. She was then referred to a charity focusing on pregnancy loss. No one at any point thought she had been pregnant.

Here, the patient's communication of having been sexually assaulted in the past, and perhaps of having been pregnant due to this, was misunderstood and responded to in a highly neglectful way. In Nadja's case, the therapist managed something different: he recognised a tendency to an excluding action – going off sick or perhaps discharging her – that was bothering him and did not simply discharge it. In inhabiting it, he in retrospect was able to see that he was in an impotent position that was similar to how Nadja had been left impotent – torn between rage towards her mother who could not help her, sympathy for her mother and shame at her anger towards her. Like in the experience of the elderly psychiatrist, he was able to find in the countertransferential experience an interpersonal drama.

It is easier to perceive these feelings in regular contact with a patient over time and harder in a more unpredictable setting or where the patient is new to the clinician. But in the case of the therapist working with Nadja, the therapist's own wellbeing is another factor that affects his capacity to perceive and respond to countertransferential feelings. If he is so burnt out that he cannot recognise that his tiredness may arise from his contact with the patient, he cannot work, and he risks responding in the rejecting way that happened with the perinatal case.

Implications and recommendations

We have argued that the active exploration of the patient's experience in all its complexity arises through its experience in the countertransference. Conscious experience of the unconscious lags behind the emotional experience, whose nature as a creation of the patient's in the mind of the therapist is hard to perceive at first. Using an example from individual therapy, we explored the complexity of countertransference in its cognitive, somatic, emotional and action-motivating aspects. By presenting examples of effective work on making sense of the countertransference, and an example of very ineffective work with it, through ignorance of it, we suggest its inevitability, power and difficulty.

Practitioners hoping to make use of their abilities effectively to use their countertransference may benefit from their own therapy to work on their ability to recognise their biases and emotional responses, as an exploratory process where they can gain an understanding of how bent out of shape they can be by their own experience. We point to the importance of tracking the manoeuvres of intersectional power, privilege and position transmitted through countertransference. No matter how uncomfortable, no matter how vulnerable and seemingly exposing, practitioners need to make use of supervision that proactively picks up on countertransference and fosters capacity to think. In addition, supervisory, reflective moments – with themselves and with colleagues – are invaluable to recognise the interpersonal drama of working with someone seeking their help may have arisen in the hard-to-metabolise internal experience of that person.

References

Bernard, V. W. (1953) Psychoanalysis and members of minority groups. *Journal of the American Psychoanalytic Association*, 1(2), 256–267. https://doi.org/10.1177/00030651 5300100203

DWDS. (2025) *"Bewältigen", prepared by das Digitale Wörterbuch der deutschen Sprache* [Database]. Available at: https://www.dwds.de/wb/bew%C3%A4ltigen (Accessed: 6th April 2025)

Freud, S. (1910) *Die zukünftigen Chancen der psychoanalytischen Therapie.* Available at: https://www.projekt-gutenberg.org/freud/kleine2/Kapitel43.html (Accessed: 6th April 2025)

Freud, S. (1912) *The Dynamics of Transference.* Volume XII The Standard Edition. London: Vintage Books.

Gabbard, G. O. (2001) A contemporary psychoanalytic model of countertransference. *Journal of Clinical Psychology*, 57, 983–991. https://doi.org/10.1002/jclp.1065

Gilbey, B. (2017) 'Too involved' or 'unable to cope': How can we bring emotions into social work? *Community Care Magazine*, 15th August 2017. https://www.communitycare.co.uk/2017/08/15/involved-unable-cope-can-bring-emotions-social-work/ (Accessed: 7th April 2025)

Heimann, P. (1950) On countertransference. *International Journal of Psychoanalysis*, 31, 81–84.

Kernberg, O. (1965) Notes on countertransference. *Journal of the American Psychoanalytic Association*, 13(1), 38–56. https://doi.org/10.1177/000306516501300102

Kernberg, O. (1987) Projection and projective identification: Developmental and clinical aspects. *Journal of the American Psychoanalytic Association*, 35(4), 795–819. https://doi.org/10.1177/000306518703500401.

Margarian, A. (2014) A cross-cultural study of somatic countertransference: A brief overview. *Asia Pacific Journal of Counselling and Psychotherapy*, 5(2), 137–145. https://doi.org/10.1080/21507686.2014.894922

McIlroy, R. (2020) Emotionally demanding. *Royal College of Nursing RCN Magazine/Bulletin*, 2nd March 2020. https://www.rcn.org.uk/magazines/Bulletin/2020/March/Emotionally-demanding (Accessed: 7th April 2025)

Nayak, S. (2021) Racialized misogyny: Response to 44th Foulkes lecture. *Group Analysis*, 54(4), 520–527. https://doi.org/10.1177/05333164211039983

Ogden, T. H. (1979) On projective identification. *International Journal of Psychoanalysis*, 60, 357–373.

Oliver, K. (2001) *Witnessing: Beyond Recognition*. Minneapolis: University of Minnesota Press.

Stein, S. (1991) The influence of theory on the psychoanalyst's countertransference. *The International Journal of Psychoanalysis*, 72(2), 325–334.

Tanzilli, A., & Lingiardi, V. (2022) The diagnostic use of countertransference in psychodynamic practice. In M. Biondi, A. Picardi, M. Pallagrosi, & L. Fonzi (Eds.), *The Clinician in the Psychiatric Diagnostic Process* (pp. 151–163). Springer Nature Switzerland AG. https://doi.org/10.1007/978-3-030-90431-9_10

Vogel, J. (2024, July 2) Use of countertransference to advance therapeutic efficacy. *American Journal of Psychotherapy*, American Psychiatric Publishing (APT), 77(4), 180–184. https://doi.org/10.1176/appi.psychotherapy.20230035

Chapter 5

The unspoken in health and social care meetings

'Group Dynamics: A Re-View'
(Bion, 1952)

Suryia Nayak and Alasdair Forrest

Introduction

Working in groups to achieve a task, goal or outcome is intrinsic to the organisation, structure and system of health and social care. Groups form the scaffolding for multidisciplinary working, groups make assessments, diagnoses, intervention/treatment plans, groups inspect, investigate and regulate. However, groups are tricky spaces, primarily because contrary to appearances, most of what goes on in them is unspoken and unconscious. The problem is that until the unspoken is made spoken and the unconscious is made conscious, groups will inevitably be held hostage to what Bion calls the three basic assumptions: dependency, pairing and fight or flight; these are unconscious defences to enable a group to disavow inevitable emotional stressors such as anxiety, fear and hatred. The problem is that whilst these feelings are allowed to play havoc, the real task of the group is stagnated, diverted and/or obscured. The spectrum of consequences can range from frustrated time/resource wasting to detrimental harm.

In this chapter, we outline how Bion's 1952 paper on the function and production of the three basic assumptions has contemporary resonance that can enable our group working to be more effective. Whilst Bion did not directly include issues of intersectional power, privilege and position, we hope that our case example and pointers, within the overview and discussion, to issues of equity, diversity and inclusion provoke thinking about how unconscious group dynamics function to sustain the status quo. We have drawn on Bion's paper to outline characteristics or conditions within groups that constitute the soil for the three basic assumptions to flourish. We then go onto summarise what each basic assumption means and how they might operate within contemporary health and social care contexts. We attempt to unpack the implications of our explanation and application of Bion's theory of basic assumption groups, concluding with recommendations for using Bion's ideas in our experiences of groups in our professional practice.

In essence, Bion invites us to shift our attention from the perceived or presenting problem to the non-problem of the group (Garland, 1982). The presenting problem is what the group sees as the task to be solved or completed, for example developing a care plan or writing a policy. The non-problem of the group is the problem

DOI: 10.4324/9781003541660-6

lurking underneath, for example, the function of being obsessed with minutes and action plans or, the habit of syphoning off tasks to sub-groups, which might seem rational and pragmatic but actually masks the non-problem or real problem of the group dynamics and feelings. This shift from the presenting problem to the non-problem involves naming the unspoken unconscious dimensions of relationships within the group and the feelings that membership of the group provokes. Bion invites us to reposition the location of disturbance. This entails a shift in the group phantasy that disturbance is all outside to facing the reality that the disturbance, the threat and the enemy are actually inside the group.

Finally, Bion's concepts are restated with the aim of providing recommendations of how a psychodynamically informed practitioner already working in health and social care settings can develop the capacities of the groups in which they actually work, rather than relying on reflective practice groups alone, which experience suggests can be difficult to start and maintain. Instead, a focus on affect and change in affect in all meetings is suggested as a way of developing a culture of better reflective use of the groups we find ourselves in within the routine work of our professional health and social care practice. By doing this, the suggestion is that the matrix of these groups – the total pool of memories, associations and meanings held unconsciously in all of our professional groups/meetings – can develop in a way that can recognise and manage the tendency towards basic assumption functioning. Here, the imperative is to keep group dynamic processes in all groups/meetings, rather than relying specifically on reflective practice groups to process the unspoken, since split off spaces, reflective practice groups/spaces can be attacked using the very basic assumption functioning Bion described, namely the threat is outside/external.

Case example

We examine Bion's paper using a case example of the kind of group interaction that characterises ordinary work in health and social care.

A care programme approach meeting was held in a low-secure forensic unit regarding a patient detained there for treatment. There was considerable anxiety about the patient's upcoming discharge, not least because of the recent CQC inspection report outcome 'requires improvement'. In attendance were a junior and a senior nurse, the patient's social worker and her student, a clinical psychologist and a junior and senior psychiatrist; the patient decided not to attend. The senior psychiatrist automatically chaired the meeting.

In the meeting, there were differing views about how quickly this discharge should happen, and how good or bad an idea it was. In spite of these differences, the meeting's anxious start gave way to quite a boring, methodical run through a CPA document and care plan. The senior psychiatrist, along with the psychologist, were very eager that the document be absolutely clear about the patient's responsibility for certain things, and very clear about the role of the housing department, which was not represented.

The junior doctor was writing busily, and the meeting stopped several times so he could be encouraged to get things just right, aware that the minutes would be referred back to when necessary. The senior psychiatrist – and in fact the social worker – agreed they would have a separate meeting to check on the care plan to ensure that it was manageable and robust against the criticism it seemed all were anxious about. The people in the meeting seemed on the one hand used to and on the other hand relieved with this separate double-checking meeting. One person said, 'We need to make sure we're covered, given CQC and that recent case in the news'.

Bearing this example in mind, we now provide an overview of Bion's paper 'Group Dynamics: A Re-View' to show the contemporary relevance of his ideas to the everyday ordinary meeting and group work within health and social care practices.

Overview of the paper

In 1952, Bion published a paper about how to understand what happens in groups in a way that has contemporary relevance for all kinds of groups in diverse health and social care contexts. This overview pulls out some of Bion's ideas that assists us to think about dynamics in groups, especially those unconscious processes that disavow the 'emotional stresses' (p. 235) held by individuals and the group as a whole in relation to the task of the group. Bion points to emotions such as panic, rage, 'anxiety, fear, hate, love and the like' (p. 236) as unspoken forces within groups because these emotions are 'are subtly affected by each other as if they were held in a combination' (p. 236). Bion is clear that the activities of the group are 'obstructed, diverted, and on occasion assisted by certain other mental activities which have in common the attribute of powerful emotional drives' (p. 235).

Bion invites us to consider what he names as the three 'basic assumptions common to all in the group' (p. 235), and these basic assumptions are inextricably linked 'instantaneous, inevitable and instinctive' (p. 235) and always present and always shifting in some shape or form. Bion states that, 'there may be two or three changes in an hour, sometimes the same basic assumption remains active for months on end' (p. 236), which points to the fact that groups can become stuck in patterns of relating and habits of decision-making and formulating plans and actions.

Before outlining how the three interrelated basic assumptions operate in groups, we outline the characteristics of groups that Bion names, which provide the conditions for the three interconnected basic assumptions to flourish. These conditions can be summarised as:

- Individual/group. Bion explains, 'the individual is a group animal at war, both with the group and with those aspects of his personality that constitute his 'groupishness' (p. 238).
- More than the sum of its members (Bion, 1952, p. 238; Dalal, 2000, p. 39). Whilst individuals play different parts in the group dynamics, we should think of the group as a whole, as a living organism (Foulkes, 1948 [1984], p. 140).

- Our 'herd' mentality. Bion states, 'there are characteristics in the individual of which the significance cannot be understood except as part of his equipment as a herd animal' (Bion, 1952, p. 239). This herd mentality shapes the group's capacity to tolerate difference, uncertainty and unfamiliarity of influence and membership.
- New ideas. New ideas provoke emotional responses which are entangled with the group's identification with the idea (i.e. good, bad, threat, protector). The group's capacity to tolerate or supress new ideas depends on the extent to which the new idea demands development and the group's capacity to tolerate that development.
- The history of the group. Here the spotlight is on the emotional stresses embedded in the historical web of communications of the group, which remain in the foundations of the group life even when the group membership changes.
- Before, during and after. The dynamics of the group, including how to manage and mask feelings towards the group task and membership, are 'in full activity before ever the group comes together in a room, although their observation may be difficult, and continue after the group has dispersed' (Bion, 1952, p. 241).
- Attitude. Bion says, 'every individual acts as if he believes that the group has an attitude to him and that it is possible to put into words what this attitude is'.
- Diversity. The capacity of a group to relate across difference correlates to the group's capacity to understand how it unconsciously manages emotional stressors: 'every human group instantaneously understands every other human group no matter how diverse in culture, language and tradition – but only within the limitations of the basic assumptions' (Bion, 1952, p. 245).

The three basic assumptions

To manage the tricky stressful conditions of groups, we resort to a set of unspoken and unconscious psychological defences that Bion calls the three basic assumptions: dependence, pairing and fight-flight. Importantly, these basic assumptions work together and are always present. It would be a mistake to believe that only one or two are ever in operation within the group. Indeed, it is not just the number of basic assumptions at play in the group but the number of people that is in the equation. Bion uses the term 'valancy' to describe the 'instantaneous involuntary combination of one individual with another for sharing and acting on a basic assumption' (p. 235). When the basic assumptions are at play, Bion refers to these as basic assumption groups.

Dependence

Bion explains that 'the group exists in order to be sustained by a leader on whom it depends for nourishment, material and spiritual, and protection' (p. 235). Here, the group looks up to the leader, legitimised by their professional and/or organisational rank and title and/or socially constructed power, privilege and position such as gender, race, class and social capital. The group becomes dependent on the leader, who is imbued with being the font of all wisdom, knowledge and deliverer of success. This dependency is shored up in the group's 'bible', documents such as minutes, action/care plans, policies, procedures and case notes/records. Dependency on the omnipotent omniscient leader has destructive consequences: the group lapses into passivity, subservience and depletion; the deified leader is bound to disappoint and fail; reification shifts to hostility; a new leader is appointed with inevitable see-sawing of all good/bad, all mad/genius splitting by those dependent on the leader.

Pairing

Bion describes 'pairing' as inevitable, to the extent that if 'the group has met for purposes of pairing' (p. 235), as if the group could not undertake the task without allocating a sub-group pairing or allowing a paring to emerge. The pairings are 'suffused with messianic hopes' of creating a genius idea or another bible. The function and sanctioning of the pairings are to relieve the group stress. A common example is where the group manages the anxiety of the problem of institutional racism and white fragility by devolving an action to the black and Asian members under the guise of their situated/lived knowledge/experience. The basic assumption applies to two people, ideas or even organisations which come together to bring a new beginning for the group or even the emergence of a messiah leading others to the proposed promised land. It is not hard to see how co-production and/or invitations to the grassroots for community-led researchers and people with lived experience could be the second basic assumption in operation.

Fight–flight

Bion explains that 'the group has met to fight something or to run away from it. It is prepared to do indifferently' (p. 235). The group takes up these binary positions for survival. Here the group is in unconscious paranoia in response to a perceived external enemy. The group phantasy is that the problem/adversary is outside of the group. In health and social care contexts, the enemy may take on guises such as constructions of risk, autonomy, capacity and liberty; the Care Quality Commission; the media; key performance indicators; data on equity diversity and inclusion failures – anything external that poses a threat to the group.

Fight mode might be manifest in cruel rants, vilification of external people, documents, systems, and passive aggressive behaviours/attitudes. Flight mode might be manifest as silence and absences, such as never getting to the key agenda item or not leaving space for the crux of the issue. Indeed, the fight–flight manoeuvre is often played out in relation to the perceived threat of reflective practice groups and spaces, where these spaces, often facilitated by someone external to the team/ward or organisation, is simultaneously viewed as both needed and threatening. Of course, external threats in all kinds of guises exist in reality, but it is the unconscious manoeuvres of the group to shift the location of disturbance outside, through fight or flight, that prevents the group's awareness that the threat is actually inside the group.

All groups, especially those that are in stagnation, would benefit from using Bion's three basic assumptions theory to enable the unspoken to be spoken, the hidden to be more visible and the emotional component that drives the group to be named.

Discussion

Bion's ideas show us a binocular view of stressful group interactions. One lens is the surface-level content of what is being discussed and what could, in a work group meeting like the one in our clinical case example, be minuted. The other, the basic assumption group, refers to the underlying relational movements and shifts in discussion that constitute a way of managing anxiety as a group as a whole. In our clinical example, things are going on that will not appear in the minutes. The group analyst Foulkes (1964) distinguished these as the manifest level and the latent level of the group, respectively.

How is this latent level accessed and made available for understanding? The psychodynamically informed practitioner needs to develop the analytic idea of 'evenly-suspended attention' (Freud, 1912), paying attention to all aspects of communication, including most prominently the affect and the sense about what seems difficult to discuss or feels avoided.

Here, the psychodynamically informed practitioner, equipped with Bion's ideas, would be attending to the underlying affect as the key guide. In our clinical example, it is not hard to see that the affect or feeling is anxiety. The anxiety is clear in the manifest-level material up for discussion: one of a discharge that clearly had clinicians worried. It is clear, though, that in the meeting, there is anxiety being handled at the latent level. Here, we can see how the latent anxiety is being via the group's defensive wish to develop certainty (where inevitable uncertainty reigns) and record things properly (which assumes the guise of the meeting's bible) but also in signs of change in feeling, mood and tone of the meeting that signal something is being managed. Initially anxious, the meeting then became devoid of anxiety: boring, methodical, and work-person-like.

Those two forms of anxiety must be distinguished because they may have very different impacts in terms of the clinical decisions made. Why were the clinicians so interested in ensuring that things were recorded so clearly? Obviously, in part there can be a sense that proper documentation helps those later reviewing a case to sympathise that the decisions were not arbitrary but instead thought-out in a transparent way. Even good decision-making, well recorded, could lead to adverse outcomes but may not be criticised because of the quality of the decision-making; this is anxiety provoking. It is also true that an agreed plan written down and clearly formulated is useful to clinicians. This goes beyond the quality of defensive health and social care where clinicians practice in a way that is greatly and anxiously conscious of the possibility of legal challenge, thus structuring their thinking accordingly (Eftekhari et al., 2023). However, Bion's work enables us to consider recorded documents in relation to a different form of anxiety; here, psychologically defended practices are about defensive avoidance of emotion rather than practising with excessive worry about criticism.

Clinicians place an excessive psychological reliance on the document to be created, which is the bible-making that Bion refers to as a dependent basic assumption. How can the clinician distinguish between the two, especially since one is essentially a realistic phenomenon whilst the other is not? Here, we suggest in our example that the affective change in the discussion, and the affective power attached to the document, are the clues.

In our example, the care plan that is being made looks on the surface to function in the service of good communication and planning – or if it is, that is not actually the primary aim of those involved. The unconscious concern is not to get the plan to be comprehensible or possible to put into effect: instead, the concern is different. The senior psychiatrist and the social worker agree to have a separate meeting to ensure that the care plan was manageable and also that it would be robust against criticism. This indicates that they did not believe that the anxiety could be contained either in the document or in the meeting – and suggests that the others in the meeting were happy with this pairing of the senior psychiatrist and the social worker rather than saying the task (with all forms of anxiety at play) could be managed in the meeting. This shows a kind of collusion with the defensive nature of the meeting. Even the senior clinicians seem to have come into a more cynical approach to the psychological problem: focusing on the document rather than the patient.

There is a strong sense of dependent group functioning, relying on leadership from the senior clinicians and also from the bible-like documents as a talisman against all criticism. It is a limited reading of Bion, though, to think that his basic assumptions are somehow different categories and that the movement between them cannot be rapid. The meeting attendees seemed reassured that the psychiatrist and social worker would go away as a saviour pair to create the perfect child: a document that comes out of this creative pairing that will do all the creating and helping.

In our example, there are a range of roles discussed. Bion wrote about valencies, which is the sense that different people in a group are psychologically primed to take on certain roles in basic-assumption functioning. For example, someone may tend to take on responsibility – allowing others to disclaim this – as a feature of their personality. In clinical settings, differential professional roles contribute in part to this valency. Here, for example, the senior psychiatrist seems to have a valency towards leadership, as is the nature of the clinical role; the junior doctor has a recording role, but as the concern arises that the junior doctor is inadequate to the task and a further defensive posture is adopted of the social worker and psychiatrist taking the document away to check it. What was not encouraged in our clinical example is a frank exchange of views, least of all with the patient, who has absented themselves.

Bion, though, tended to see a distilled view of groups that was about their essential elements rather than one that is more clearly rooted in the social nature of persons. For example, the differences in power and professional or other authority in a group between members were not a focus of his concern; the bigger focus was on the differentiation between leader and members as a whole. This is a limit in his analysis. Group analytic writers like Dalal (1998) and many others have placed in the foreground the issues of intersectional differential power relationships in a way that brings analytic group thinking closer to the broader literature on social processes. Aiyegbusi (2024) has done this in particular in relation to professional groups in the UK National Health Service.

Bion's distilled view of groups also limited his ability to consider the full organisational and social context of groups. In this example, there is concern that comes from the contemporary practice environment of the clinicians but also a concern related to the public profile of adverse incidents. In our example, one person in the meeting refers to a recent case in the news.

This is a realistic concern: Kongara et al. (2024), surveying psychiatrists in the United Kingdom who were under investigation following an adverse incident, found significant psychological distress and life changes related to being under such investigation. The psychodynamic practitioner is not concerned with ignoring institutional or professional reality. However, a focus on the defensive management of anxiety will limit the discussion, limit the realistic focus of the meeting and close off possibilities for a more creative or nuanced approach. Bion, who was a tank commander during the First World War, knew that it would be hard to think when under fire beyond thinking in basic survival terms.

A contemporary group analytic practitioner would also be curious about other valencies, including the intersectional identity of the patient. The patient's identity here is constituted by being a patient in a secure unit, and by being an offender, but it will also be constituted by power relationships relating to age, gender, stereotypes of particular groups, the patient's social affiliations and their diagnosis. It will be constituted by that important forensic psychiatric concern: the axis between "madness" and "badness".

What could the psychodynamic practitioner do here? They could make an interpretation, but like the most helpful interpretations, one that does not look like an interpretation. We suggest that a helpful intervention would have been to recognise the anxiety and say that there was clearly a need for a good care plan and that it was a priority to draft one. That said, we suggest that the meeting was at risk of feeling under fire and could put too much faith in a care plan. How can the attendees get a chance to contribute and think together more freely, and keep the focus on the patient's needs, whilst respecting that need? We suggest there would be greater need to hear from everyone and give everyone a chance to speak especially about things they felt reluctant to address. We might suggest that the best chair of the meeting would be someone who is most experienced in these situations; alternatively, we might suggest the best chair would be someone with the least need to contribute to the future care plan, so they could help others have the space to think.

That would not be likely to solve the problem, though. We would probably try to notice the shifts into very anxious thinking that had a basic-assumption quality to it and notice that as a meeting we were getting more anxious or frantic and ask what was inspiring that at that point. We would probably try to discourage the idea that another meeting could somehow solve this meeting's problems and ask if we may not need to prolong this meeting a little to agree something now rather than prematurely reassuring ourselves with this kind of delegation – even to those in a leadership role. If we thought a recent case in the news was probably inspiring anxiety but it was being hinted at, we would advocate openly mentioning it.

The aim of this work by the psychodynamic practitioner would not be to abolish anxiety: this is clearly an anxious situation. The aim would be to promote thinking in a realistic way, including anxiety, without the use of highly defensive group movements into dependency, fight-or-flight or pairing. We would always tend to be suspicious of bible-making and would distinguish that from realistic planning, or even from defensive medicine or its equivalent in other professions.

Implications and recommendations

Having considered the example with the concepts from Bion but with a renewed emphasis on affect, we use the principles drawn out from the paper to develop recommendations for how a psychodynamically oriented practitioner in health and social care could manage and make use of group-dynamic processes:

- Individual/group tension. The psychodynamically aware practitioner would think about this conflict between persons' essentially group-related nature and their individuality as part of what is expected in group interactions. In a care programme approach meeting, or in a ward round, basic assumption functioning is to be expected and understood rather than defensively colluded with. By doing that, we are able to anticipate and manage the development of a discourse about a patient, a client or an organisation that is unable to see the totality of what is going on.
- The group is more than, or other than, the sum of its members. This links to Bion's other idea about the importance of the history of the group. By recognising that groups take on a life of their own, with their own characteristics that have their own history and development, we can avoid the idea that we are unconstrained actors. Foulkes (1948 [1984]) developed this using the concept of the matrix. This was the idea that there was a common set of norms, assumptions, a shared memory and history and shared ideas of what potential there is and is not, in a group – and that it lives on in the group. We shall return to this later.
- Our herd mentality. Bion's idea is that we have a tendency towards some kind of superficial intragroup cohesion and tend to divest ourselves of authority and lodge it in a particular person and then see this as so essential to human nature that we need to accommodate ourselves to it. In health and social care, the psychodynamic practitioner would recognise and accept this tendency, whilst

thinking about times when its strictures prevent creativity in thought and action and may then feel a need for a leadership role in promoting different capacities for thinking.

- New ideas. New ideas threaten the group's previous ways of working, and groups have a capacity to tolerate this that differs at different times and in different groups. The thoughtful practitioner may need to take the temperature of the group and be realistic about what new ideas are manageable or what the defensive response may be to ideas that are not.
- Before, during and after. Bion's idea that the dynamics of the group are in effect before it meets, whilst it meets, and after it meets reminds us that groups are not just physical collections but shared psychological phenomena. A practitioner who thinks that the purpose of a meeting is the meeting itself misses the substrate of the interpersonal processes at play during it and does not recognise that much of the interaction has already happened consciously and unconsciously in the minds of the members of the group and continues long after. As group analysts, we often find patients saying their weekly group therapy begins days before when they start to think of the group and continues for days afterwards. It develops in the context of the matrix of the group.
- Attitude. When Bion writes of a person acting as though the group has an attitude towards them already, he reminds us that interactions between people are not unmediated, direct interactions but rather come through transferences but also that it is possible to have a transferential relationship with a whole group and have unconscious and conscious expectations of how one will be received in a group, including in this group.
- Diversity. Bion thought the capacity of the group to relate to diversity correlated with its ability to manage basic assumption functioning. The psychodynamic practitioner would recognise the profound defensive processes that can be awakened by diversity of background, thought or role and try to manage the defensive processes to allow for the development of a group culture that values such difference.

Much of Bion's work hints, as we have written, at the idea of a shared psychological space and heritage in a group but in words that he did not translate into concrete terminology. Foulkes (1964), though, termed this 'the matrix'. In our case example, the matrix of the group could be seen in the shared understanding, unconsciously arrived at and held, of who speaks first, who can say what and how the meeting should be structured – as well as memory of what has and has not worked in the past, how previous such meetings have been, and what the organisational context is. It would include the personal and professional histories of those there, and the memory in the institution that previous psychiatrists held CPAs in a different way. It is not separate from the culture, or even the news here. It is that common pool of associations and meaning.

Whilst every group has an inevitable tendency towards defensively moving into basic assumption functioning and can make rapid shifts in this regard, Bion's work suggests that such functioning can become highly engrained in a way that becomes part of the matrix of the group and constrains a reasonable understanding of the nature of anxiety, defeating the group's ability to handle a task. Here, this is an anxious situation. In our example, if the group always relies on the pairing between the psychiatrist and social worker to sort out its problems, then it cannot manage problems without them, manage problems they cannot manage, or manage problems in a different way than their particular skills and potentially then rigidified approach would allow. If the group/meeting always relies on bible-making to generate a document that means so much in and of itself, it will struggle to engage meaningfully with the problem at hand, prioritising the document. A human interaction becomes, 'we need to run through this paperwork' as though the paperwork were the goal.

The usual suggestion about groups like this is that they should have reflective practice with an external facilitator. The difficulty is that repeated experience shows that to be difficult to establish and difficult to sustain. There are pragmatic reasons for this related to the priority given to urgent work, inadequate staffing and the wider economic and political drivers. There are also defensive reasons related to Bion's ideas that groups struggle to tolerate new ideas, diversity, and challenge, and resort to a fight-or-flight basic assumption that portrays the external facilitator as a threat.

Instead, though, using Bion's ideas, a psychodynamically informed practitioner working already in such a setting may get a sense of how affect is managed in the group and find it is too defensive to allow for this open attack on the defences that reflective practice could entail. They might, and the organisation might, seek to improve the reflective functioning of meetings and groups already in use. Here, the CPA meeting could be used to reflect on the case of the patient – and ideally with the patient – if the basic assumption functioning is understood and, by being gently named in meaningful ways, the capacity of the meeting – and the matrix of the combined set of such meetings in the organisation – could be changed.

In this discussion, we suggest that the practitioner could both acknowledge the importance of the document and also recognise that its role in actually managing the situation is limited. When that idea catches on in the next CPA for another patient or the CPA after that, or when others recognise that in themselves in time, the matrix of the group does change. If, say, the social worker has been saying, 'the psychiatrist and I don't have special answers in our special post-CPA meetings', and the nurse smiles, and then it gets said again in a different way in the next CPA, and that becomes the social worker's catchphrase, that demonstrates the reflective capacity of the group. If the junior psychiatrist says that they had similar anxious ward rounds in a different placement, that suddenly felt less anxious, but then something bad happened, that also develops the capacity of the group. Whilst reflective practice groups get seen as a gold standard, if they contain fewer members of the team – albeit able to reflect in a less structured way that may promote more creative discussion – are they more useful as a forum than groups that contain the whole team?

This improved attention to the reflective capacities of meetings already in use may throw up more questions for the practitioner than it answers – but possibly fruitful ones. Why does the nurse always speak second? Is there a difference in whose voice can be heard – and whose voice carries more importance? In the case example, we have not included information about the intersecting identities of the professionals involved, only their profession and for some their seniority in it. If the nurse is a black woman with recent experience of immigration to the country, what is her valency for the particular roles she will be placed in by the group? Is there any reason why the overall patterns of relatedness in society – which are gendered and racialised patterns – would not restate themselves in this group, and how will their being restated be managed? These questions – which have an urgency to them in any group – are all the more difficult to manage if, as Bion indicates, the group is set at a level of functioning where basic assumption functioning is engrained as the constant manoeuvre in the group and it overwhelms other capacities for functioning.

It is only if these are worked on that a most urgent question in the case example can be dealt with: why is the patient not there? Are there constrained ways of relating that prevent the patient from joining? How much of the responsibility for that lies with him and how much with the staff group? Can there be creative thought about this? What about the intersecting identities of the patient; are they relevant to this if he is, for example, a mixed-race man without children, who is single, who has schizophrenia and who has a diagnosis of personality disorder and a history of drug use? How can these intersecting axes of identity, and how they fit into structures of power and exclusion, be recognised and their understanding incorporated into the work of the group in a way that allows for his voice to be heard?

Conclusion

In summary, we suggest that Bion's ideas are about taking a perspective on groups that sees them as what they are: groups, not collections of individuals. They evoke in group members, and employ as a group in and of itself, defensive manoeuvres against anxiety that are not exact analogies of the defensive manoeuvres seen in individual psychology. To be worked with – and indeed in – they need to be understood on their own, group-oriented basis. That involves understanding that groups can rely on divesting authority from others and placing them in a leader or leadership function like a constructed bible, can rely on the development of something creative between two people as the only way of managing anxiety or can rely on creating a fight-or-flight atmosphere. All of these constrain the development of what Bion called a work group but which we prefer to see as a matrix of the group. In time, with attention to the affect in a group as the primary clue to the functioning of the group, a group's capacities can change, and the matrix develop into one more able to be reflective and able to attend to the nature of what happens in the group.

References

Aiyegbusi, A. (2024) Holding the Broken Pieces: An Intersectional Approach to Group Analysis for Women in Prison. Chapter in: Nayak, S. & Forrest, A. (Eds.) *Intersectionality and Group Analysis.* London: Routledge. pp. 26–47.

Bion, W. (1952) Group Dynamics: A Re-View. *The International Journal of Psychoanalysis*, 33, 235–247.

Dalal, F. (1998) *Taking the Group Seriously: Towards a Post-Foulkesian Group Analytic Theory*. London: Jessica Kingsley.

Dalal, F. (2000) *Taking the Group Seriously: Towards a Post-Foulkesian Group Analytic Theory*. London: Jessica Kingsley Publishers.

Eftekhari, M. H., Parsapoor, A., Ahmadi, A., *et al.* (2023) Exploring Defensive Medicine: Examples, Underlying and Contextual Factors, and Potential Strategies – a Qualitative Study. *BMC Medical Ethics*, 24, 82.

Foulkes, S. H. (1948 [1984]) *Introduction to Group-Analytic Psychotherapy: Studies in the Social Interaction of Individuals and Groups*. London: Karnac [Original publication, London: Heinemann].

Foulkes, S. H. (1964) *Therapeutic Group Analysis*. London: Allen and Unwin [Reprinted London: Karnac, 1984].

Freud, S. (transl. Strachey, J.) (1912) Recommendations to Physicians Practising Psycho-Analysis. *The Standard Edition of the Complete Psychological Works of Sigmund Freud, Volume XII (1911–1913): The Case of Schreber, Papers on Technique and Other Works.* pp. 109–120.

Garland, C. (1982) Group-Analysis: Taking the Non-Problem Seriously. *Group Analysis*, 15(1), 4–14.

Kongara, S., Tamworth, M., & Gibbons, R. (2024) Experiences and Support Needs of Psychiatrists Under Investigation. *BJPsych Bulletin*, 1–8.

Chapter 6

Leading, following and mentoring through the lens of 'Envy and Gratitude' (Klein, 1957)

Shelly Allen and Naomi Sharples

Introduction

The idea for this chapter came from a discussion of providing mentorship to a leader who was struggling to make sense of the dynamics between himself and two members of the team. The description of the unsettling dynamic was rich, even when being relayed between us as one providing mentorship and the other offering a reflective space to think about it. It was evocative and lively with visual imagery, and thinking about it together, we saw it as an opportunity to consider how to support the mentee/mentor relationship through an exploration of the relational dynamics between the leader and the team members as a considered case example.

To begin with we started from the premise of jealousy evoked by professional rivalry, but as our discussion progressed, this felt like a less convincing position. There was not an obvious desire, consciously at least, expressed by the two team members to usurp the leader and take their place. That said, it needed to be kept in mind because we did not have sufficient understanding to rule it out. We also acknowledged that unconscious desires can be kept at bay through taking up an opposite position, in psychodynamic approaches this is referred to as reaction formation, much like claiming not to care about the possibility of promotion as a way of managing this desire and potential disappointment if it did not come to fruition.

We thought that the paper 'Envy and Gratitude' (Klein, 1957) might help us to think about the relational dynamics more deeply through reflection on what we were noticing in our discussions together. We thought it might help to underpin the work of mentorship with the leader who expressed concern that they felt stuck and pressured.

Initially we came to understand the relational dynamics to include a refusal to take up the nourishment being offered, and further, a wish to destroy and spoil the leader's efforts to support the two team members. We contrasted this with the mentor's experience of working with the mentee, who had been thankful of the time and space to think about the complexity of their work, which we understood to have felt containing with elements of well-intentioned challenge in an effort to support leadership development.

DOI: 10.4324/9781003541660-7

What follows is a case example to reflect the work between the mentor and mentee; it is adapted for confidentiality, but crucially maintains the dynamic we have described. We will then link this with an overview of 'Envy and Gratitude' to show how this paper offered a helpful framework through which to consider the issues and assist the mentor in their support of the mentee.

To begin with, we want to offer something relating to language. It has been noted that difficulties arise when using everyday words that are familiar, such as envy, as technical terms (Bott Spillius et al., 2011). We will be mindful of this when trying to relate the essence of Klein's paper within this chapter and offer this clarification from the outset to set the scene and signpost. Envy as we understand it here and in line with Klein's paper, concerns two-person relationships in which there is a desire to take away and spoil what the other has. It is hatred oriented, whilst jealousy involves relationships beyond a dyad of two people; it is love oriented and derives from the feeling of having something that is due, taken away by a rival.

We will then go on to discuss and expand the ideas proposed to show how Klein gave the opportunity to think deeply about what might be happening in the dynamic between the leader who had sought mentorship and their team members. Implications and recommendations will follow with a view to offering some thoughts regarding the dynamics that existed within the leader and follower relationship and in relation to the mentor/mentee. We think there are elements that will be familiar to others and that this has transferability beyond this specific case example through reflection on one's own experiences and observations.

In maintaining confidentiality, the following case example does not aim to depict a factual account. It is not the intention to 'prove that really happened' but instead to illustrate how 'Envy and Gratitude' helped the mentor in trying to understand the complex dynamics between the leader they were supporting as mentee and members of the team.

Case example

Jon is one of a group of heads of division in a busy clinical environment; each head is managed by a clinical director. Jon manages 14 staff.

Over the past four years, his relationship with his team has moved from a junior clinician working with them to head of their division. Outwardly, the transition has appeared easy for some staff, but for others it seemed to be more challenging. Jon is new to leadership and keen to understand his areas of leadership competence and strength as well as areas he finds more challenging. As part of his own development, he engages in a mentor/mentee relationship with a senior colleague who is experienced in leading, leadership theory, leader development and reflection.

During mentorship, Jon described an increasing sense of being manipulated by two members of the team, one a younger member, Simon, who was pulling Jon into what was felt to be an unnecessary level of detail of his work; Simon was requesting help but at the same time not taking up the wider organisational support available, and his disengagement spread to the individual support offered by Jon.

Jon in turn felt frustrated, 'not good enough', a sense of being pulled into Simon's anxiety, drawn into his chaotic work experience then pushed away and rejected as a poor leader. The pulling and pushing, the being drawn in and then rejected, offering help only to have the help ignored, was creating feelings of frustration, anger and inadequacy in Jon. The resulting impact on Simon's clinical work was evident, and this added work for Jon because he had to constantly double check Simon's quality of work and reduce the 'ask' of him.

The second member of staff was presented in the mentorship discussions as the antithesis of Simon. Paula, a senior member of the team with years of clinical experience, would seek Jon out to offer her advice, guidance, feedback and judgement on his ability as a head of division and as a clinician. In offering her knowledge and experience, Jon felt that Paula left little space in the relationship for him to negotiate issues such as caseloads, case reviews and organisational expectations. If he tried to raise these issues with Paula, he would be met with a slew of detailed feedback on his own performance, what he should be focusing on, how he was being 'played' by 'management' and what he needed to do instead. Jon reflected on his understanding that Paula had never chosen to become a manager but wanted to offer constant leadership coaching to him from her position of clinical experience and organisational longevity. Jon found himself being pulled away from the work he needed Paula to focus on; he described her unsolicited advice as being like a fog, covering everything and making it hard to see the detail. Judgement and feedback made him feel like he was being played like a puppet with Paula as a very skilled and disparaging puppeteer.

Having set the scene, we will now offer an overview of Klein (1957); it is worth saying that it is a rich paper, as is typical of her work. As Likierman (2015) comments, Melanie Klein's work is impressive, an original contribution to our understanding of the human condition. This contribution has been wide ranging, Klein's theory, termed object relations and which was developed further by others, takes a premise that will be very familiar to those who work in health and social care. This relates to an infant being sensitive to their environment, particularly the maternal emotional attitude, and that loving parental care in early life lays the ground for adult mental health (Likierman, 2015). This proposal, that early experiences influence health and wellbeing in adult life, is seldom disputed. That said, there are aspects of Klein's underpinning principles of object relations that are not wholeheartedly endorsed: 'her critics feel that . . . her vision is inappropriately negative and pessimistic about human nature' (Likierman, 2015, p. 4). This mixed reception to Klein's ideas is exemplified by the response to 'Envy and Gratitude' (Klein, 1957) and we will attempt to reflect aspects of this as follows.

Overview of the paper

'Envy and Gratitude' was one of Melanie Klein's key contributions as an original piece of psychoanalytic work; it was published during the latter period of her life in 1957. This was two years after first presenting the key ideas at the 1955

International Psychoanalytic Congress, and it was not without controversy: 'this more established status did not guarantee a universal acceptance or even tolerance of Klein's thinking, because far from mellowing over time, her ideas seemed to have reached a new extremity' (Likierman, 2015, p. 172).

This controversy is linked to Klein's assertion that envy is innate, operating from birth, and typifies destructive impulses rather than arising as the baby develops and gains increasing maturity. Critics found this pessimistic and unrealistic, a step too far to think that a baby starts life with the most anti-social of the seven deadly sins (Likierman, 2015). Despite the controversy aroused in relation to 'Envy and Gratitude', it is said to have led to important developments in psychoanalytic understanding and to be of great clinical significance (Roth, 2008).

'Envy and Gratitude' is a rich and complicated paper which brings many of Klein's key concepts together. For this overview, we have had to privilege some aspects over others in illustrating how we used it to understand issues reflected in the case example. As such, we do not claim that this is an exhaustive consideration of the paper. Rather, we intend to show how the application of classic psychoanalytic papers can offer a depth of consideration to the issues that trouble contemporary health and social care.

Klein (1957) starts the paper with her statement of interest: early experiences of envy and gratitude. Envy is the most powerful factor that undermines love and gratitude because it affects the earliest relationship of all, that with the mother. This unconscious, primary envy, which underlies all other types, is a key concept of the paper. Klein compares and contrasts her work with that of Freud including the life and death instincts and drives, and she later makes mention of penis envy. Abraham's contribution is also remarked upon, and Klein notes her satisfaction in being able to contribute to the recognition of Abraham's discoveries so many years after his death but also the differences. In keeping with the point made previously, this is when envy and hostility arise in an individual, which for Abraham is later than Klein's proposal that it operates from the beginning of life.

Typically, given Klein's focus on the early life of infants, the relationship between this period of emotional life and mental health in adulthood is key in 'Envy and Gratitude'. Of this, Klein (1957) states that the adult can only be understood in relation to the baby and then followed up in adulthood. This to-and-fro between adult and babyhood is expressed within the transference to the analyst, transference being the direction of feelings, desires and phantasies from formative relationships such as with parents, onto the therapist.

The importance of the mother as the infant's first object, this being the mental representation that is internalized through introjection by the infant, which is a blueprint for development, is stressed in Klein (1957). If, through this mechanism of introjection, the mother's breast which feeds and nourishes the baby, and in later development the mother as a whole, becomes secure in the ego, this forms a satisfactory foundation for development. She proposes that eventually, this is experienced as life and then love itself: 'the good breast is taken in and becomes part of the ego, and the infant who was first inside the mother now has the mother inside himself' (Klein, 1957, p. 179).

The role that external circumstance plays in relation to introjection of the mother is then explained in relation to its impact on the internalization of the good breast. The to-and-fro we mentioned is then related to the early emotional life of the infant who loses and regains the good object, the breast, and the later mental representation of the mother, through being fed and nourished but also experiences frustration and dread when this nourishment is absent. It should be noted that Klein is at pains to say that this is not just related to physical nourishment: the breast is a prototype of goodness, patience, generosity and creativity.

Envy is linked here through being deprived of the gratification gained from the good object, which in 'Envy and Gratitude' is experienced as being kept for itself and causing frustration for the infant. The first object to be envied is the feeding breast, but Klein takes this further when considering problematic circumstances such as difficulties during birth and adapting to the post-natal world. Problematic experiences such as these mean that the baby starts at a disadvantage. Envy is not just related to such circumstances in Klein's theory; it is also said to be constitutional in part, thereby relating to the controversy mentioned previously about envy operating from the beginning of life.

It is in being able to be successfully fed and cared for by the mother, who enjoys this role with her baby, that nourishment can be accepted and enjoyed by the infant. With this, the good breast is internalized, which consequently impacts the development of gratitude and happiness. Essentially good experiences of being cared for allow the baby to experience the world as caring and nourishing; this is then internally represented in the psyche of the baby, providing a foundation from which further development ensues. Poor experiences also impact development, and this is significant for the paper in how envy then manifests.

Distinctions are made between envy, jealousy and greed, with Klein offering the explanation that envy is an angry response that another possesses something that is wanted, the impulse being to take it away and/or spoil it. Envy is mostly associated with projection and greed, introjection, an insatiable taking in of something. Jealousy, based on envy, differs in that it relates to at least two people and is associated with love that is felt to be warranted and is at risk of being taken away.

A particularly pertinent aspect for this chapter is the interplay between greed, envy and persecutory anxiety, which Klein (1957) states are all linked: when one increases, so do the others in a perpetuating cycle. However, with the establishment of a good object, a child can withstand temporary states of envy without permanent damage; it is transient, and when the good object can be regained again and again, this is crucial in laying a foundation of stability and a strong ego.

Gratitude is linked to love in the paper; it underlies an appreciation of what is good in the self and others. It is linked to trust in good figures and allows what is referred to as gifts, that are gained through assimilating trusted good figures, which can then be shared with others. This makes introjection of a friendly external world possible, and the more gratification results from the breast, the more frequent enjoyment and gratitude are experienced. This repeated experience plays a part in the ability to make reparation, with inner wealth shared and re-introjected, which is enriching.

Where Klein states that envy is in part constitutional, she acknowledges that it is an emotion which will be roused in all, but the strength of it and its management are particular to the individual. It plays a part in why the capacity for enjoyment, linked to gratitude for what has been received, also differs in individuals. Links between envy and guilt are considered, and Klein gives examples of ways to rouse envy such as ambition and the relative absence of envy in others. The confidence in one's own creativity is said to counteract envy, and constructive criticism is referred to in helping to further another's work. Defence mechanisms against envy are considered in the paper, and Klein includes several clinical examples to illustrate the points presented before concluding.

We will now identify aspects of the paper that we found to be pertinent to the case example and draw these out further in the discussion that follows.

Discussion

As stated in the introduction, the key focus for our discussion in this chapter is leadership and followership and the exploration of these experiences through a mentor/mentee relationship. Through our reflections prompted by 'Envy and Gratitude' (Klein, 1957), we use a psychodynamic approach to understanding the issues included in the case example. We take inspiration from the proposal that understanding the dynamics of teams can lead to meaningful action and changes, with a more mature approach to the task (Cardona, 2020).

The refusal of nourishment

One of Jon's frustrations was that Simon would not take up the offer of support, refusing to take it in and make use of it. In our reflections, we likened this to early experiences of feeding and being able to take in the mother's milk. Jon was perplexed at Simon's refusal of support; to him it did not make sense. Klein's thinking on envy is that it operates from the beginning of life, and in the beginning, it is in relation to the breast. For anyone who has experience of feeding babies, it is not necessarily straightforward; sometimes the milk goes in, and if it mostly stays in, the baby is satisfied for now. At other times, no amount of cajoling, coaxing and encouraging achieves the aim of a fed, content baby. The milk seeps from the mouth; anxiety in the caregiver rises that not enough feed is being taken in to nourish and sustain the baby. The shrill cries of protestation, and at times pain inflicted on the mother's body, make an emotionally charged experience even more difficult. The very thing, the breast or bottle and its milk, that the baby needs to survive, grow and develop, is being refused.

Envy, according to Klein, is in part constitutional and is modified by environmental factors such as adversity: 'the first good object has a unique place in mental life, as it does throughout the life cycle, since the human individual continues to depend on the self-nourishing, creative core, that was introjected in infancy' (Likierman, 2015, p. 173). Whilst we do not want to offer ill-conceived notions about the early lives of Jon and Simon, being open to wondering about them allows a reflective space to be taken up and assist in moving from a position of 'I just don't understand' to one of 'there may be reasons why it's like this.'

As stated, for Klein, envy is anger that another person possesses something desirable with the associated wish to ruin and spoil it. Jon hinted at this through feelings of not being good enough as a leader; no matter what he offered, it was felt to be spoilt and disregarded. It can be difficult for leaders to understand why their best efforts are not having the desired effect, just like the caregiver offering the baby their milk, but by posing the leader–follower relationship as a dynamic impacted upon by a multitude of influences, it becomes possible to open something up for consideration.

This point is made by (Cardona, 2020), who says that understanding the link between difficulties at work and our early experiences can have a transformative effect by offering the opportunity to moderate the effect of past difficulties and help manage in a more meaningful and effective way (Cardona, 2020). It is important to stress here that using this idea as a defensive manoeuvre is not what we are advocating. It is not a way to relinquish responsibility as a leader by claiming the problem is all in the team member's childhood. Instead, we see this as a way of appreciating the complexity of what we all bring to the work situation and an appreciation of this can help with being more resourceful when trying to understand the inevitably challenging dynamics at play.

In drawing on the idea of envy as Klein understood it, it is possible to hypothesise that there is something significant in the feeling that no matter what one does as a leader it is not good enough. The risk of this is to disengage, but by gaining an appreciation that this is a much more complex dynamic, it makes it possible to wonder and approach it with a sense of curiosity. If straightforward attempts at offering support are ruined, what other modes can be employed which might prove more fruitful? To return to the idea of the feeding baby, is there a particular way of holding them that makes feeding more successful? Timing may be crucial, or a pattern may exist that reveals something of the need to offer certain types of nourishment in a well-timed and thoughtful way.

With time and reflection, it may be possible to put words to a hypothesis that can be shared and explored, providing this is with caution, due regard and positive intention. We view this through the use of quality mentorship that is intent on helping the mentee to take a reflective stance to their work. In doing, it may enable the movement from a lack of understanding to being open to the possibility that there may be reasons why a team member behaves as they do towards the leader. This is situated in the dynamic between people, in our example Jon and Simon both bringing their own experiences to this relationship. This is summed up by Obholzer (2021) who points out that it is 'advisable in one's adult role to give some thought to how we came to be the way we are, and to use that insight to build on our strengths and assets, but also keep an eye on our vulnerabilities' (p. 11).

The disparaging puppeteer

Our second key theme derives from Jon's feeling of being manipulated and links to one of Melanie Klein's significant contributions to psychoanalytic theory in understanding the psyche, termed projective identification. This is an unconscious process where aspects of the self are split off and attributed externally; commonly another person who may then take up this projection through identification with it. This may seem outlandish, but an everyday example can help to show it is not as strange as it may seem.

A team member is anxious about their work performance, they find it hard to bear this level of anxiety and concern that they are not functioning effectively. The inability to bear this anxiety about performance is split off and projected onto the leader. They are then related to by the team member in a critical way, as if they are doing a bad job. If the leader is susceptible to this unconscious communication, they may pick up on this feeling that they are a poor leader, undermining them and raising their anxiety. This may then manifest in areas such as indecisiveness, withdrawal from being able to support the team, thereby confirming the team members experience of them, the projection has been identified with.

We can understand Jon's feelings of being manipulated drawing on this concept of projective identification, although it is important to note that it is also crucial not to be dismissive of a complaint that the leader is not effective; it is in keeping an open mind to all possibilities that the mentor can be most resourceful.

With distance from the actual situation, and with space to reflect on it and the impression of Jon as a leader in so far as it can be known in the mentor/mentee relationship, the mentor has been able to consider whether Paula is frustrated that her years of clinical expertise and knowledge of the organisation have not been put to good use. Rather than being able to face the pain of this, there is a possibility that Paula has split this off and projected into Jon, his identification with it. And whilst this is not guaranteed, in Jon's situation, he did feel like he was lacking in his leadership and organisational knowledge; the risk then is that he starts behaving as if he is not good enough in his role. This process relieves Paula of this difficult feeling; she is now free from it, and whilst Jon's confidence is undermined, this confirms what Paula thought all along.

There is a potential link here to the perpetuating cycle that Klein describes as envy, guilt and persecutory anxiety, all of which increase each other. Without being able to explore and work through what is happening with skilled others, there is a risk of nothing changing or worse, Jon's performance at work deteriorating and consequently impacting team functioning. However, through the mentorship relationship, Jon was able to articulate his experiences of the disparaging puppeteer and reflect in a more reality-based way on aspects of leadership and where he has strengths and areas for development.

By enabling this reality-based position and putting it into words, the opportunity is created to recognise feelings of inadequacy when working with Paula and allow himself the space to try to think and make conscious choices, rather than being drawn, without conscious awareness, into a position that relieves Paula of her own anxieties. This might not be consistently successful, projective identification can be powerful to resist, particularly if there is an existing vulnerability to the projection, but knowledge of its sway can also help to be prepared for it.

Ambition is also an area that Klein equates with envy and gratitude; we do not know enough about Paula's unconscious motives in relation to Jon to pose credible possibilities. Expressly, there has not been a desire to be leader but thinking about the circumstances of their interactions together, we cannot rule it out with certainty either. Knowing that people are under the sway of their unconscious is both unsettling and potentially resourceful, it means we can move away from efforts to rationally explain something to a position that accounts for a more relational approach. This links to being psychologically present and is key to the functioning, development and stability of staff (Cardona, 2020). It has three essential conditions: not being preoccupied with one's own issues, being involved in meaningful tasks at work and feeling safe enough to be oneself without fear of negative consequences (Cardona, 2020).

Our propensity towards envy is said to be laid down in our early life:

In contrast with the infant who, owing to his envy, has been unable to build up securely a good internal object, a child with a strong capacity for love and gratitude has a deep rooted relation with a good object and can, without being fundamentally damaged, withstand temporary states of envy, hatred and grievance, which arise in children who are loved and well mothered.

(Klein, 1957, p. 187)

This links to our capacity for work and organisational life, which is informed by early experiences; it follows that without a degree of emotional attachment to a meaningful activity, work can feel meaningless and impact fulfilment (Cardona, 2020). Considering this in relation to Paula may offer some potential avenues to explore. Longevity and organisational memory offer a unique contribution to the work: it can be surmised that something and/or someone is keeping Paula employed in this organisation despite the grievance Jon experiences. This poses questions as to how then this can be understood, and again, 'Envy and Gratitude' can be drawn on in this context.

Klein (1957) describes the dynamic between analyst and analysand – the person in analysis – where something helpful has been offered by the analyst only to be denigrated and criticised later. Having an understanding that in certain circumstances, a leader's best efforts will be responded to in this way may allow curiosity about it rather than despondency to prevail. Whilst we would not claim to understand Paula and Jon in terms of early developmental perspectives, we can be curious about their relationship, the dynamic between them and Klein's contentions about envy.

What of gratitude?

Our key theme starts with acknowledgement that the 1957 paper was the first time Melanie Klein put envy and gratitude together. Whilst envy gets more attention in her writing, gratitude has a significant place in Klein's theories and here in proposing an understanding of the dynamics shared through the case example. Klein (1957) sees gratitude as having a constitutional basis just as envy which is influenced by the environment. To share gratitude, for Klein, is an expression of love which strengthens the personality and helps recover from states of hatred (Bott Spillius et al., 2011). For instance, through mentorship Jon was afforded an attentive, interested other, intent on trying to use their mind and experience in teasing out key aspects of his perplexing experiences with the aim of assisting him to understand and bear it.

As stated previously, Klein has made a significant contribution to how we understand the importance of early emotional life in relation to development and wellbeing as adults. Our understanding of the importance of this has been progressed through the significant contributions of Melanie Klein and others which we will draw on here.

The baby needs a receptive caregiver to help manage. This links to Wilfred Bion's concept of container–contained (Bion, 1962), where the 'good enough mother' (Winnicott, 1953) provides the baby with an experience of containing their anxiety, showing it can be managed and with repeated experiences; this is how the baby comes to know that this raw anxiety which threatens to overwhelm can be dealt with. It requires a balance between not too much, as in not so overprotective that the baby's development is inhibited, and not too little so that the baby feels out of its depth and unable to manage the terror of their experiences.

This relates as much to professional relationships as personal ones; a containing mentorship relationship has much in common with these early experiences and links to Britton's (2004) concept of a 'third position'. This is a mental space from which the subjective self can be observed having a relationship to an idea. Britton says subjective belief comes first followed by objective evaluation, and the third position requires an integration of the subjective with the objective, thereby enabling self-observation. This can be seen as a consequence of the mentorship relationship and has the potential to help Jon, as a leader, to provide containment and support to his team whilst being able to tolerate negative projections from staff as well as people using the service (Cardona, 2020).

This links to Klein's understanding of how reparation fits with envy and gratitude: by being supported in an informed, containing and good enough way, it is possible that Jon can be more able to bear the spoiling of his efforts by Simon and Paula without retaliation. As stated in 'Envy and Gratitude', confidence in one's own creativity, which we see as the mentorship relationship having been important in establishing this, counteracts envy, and where constructive criticism aims to support the development of the work, we can also see Klein's contention of the motherly and fatherly attitude being pertinent in the mentorship relationship. The mentor moving between an empathic position and a more objective stance, this to-and-fro being referred to in the context of the psychoanalyst and patient as representative of the maternal and paternal roles (Bateman & Holmes, 2008).

Implications and recommendations

In this section, we take our reflections from the case example and discussion to suggest how the application of psychodynamic approaches inspired by 'Envy and Gratitude' may be helpful in terms of leadership, teams and organisations.

Valuing early experiences

In keeping with one of the main tenets of Melanie Klein's vast contribution to psychodynamic theory, we start by stressing that a developmental perspective has much to offer in relation to working relationships and environments that provide health and social care.

Understanding the importance of relational dynamics at work, on which psychodynamic approaches have much to say, enables a framework and language to engage in reflection in an attempt to enhance understanding. Having an appreciation of the role that early experiences have in our work relationships, our use of processes and engagement with systems assists with this.

Forming attachments and containing structures is crucial for healthy and meaningful engagement with work (Cardona, 2020). In much the same way as the baby needs caregivers who are attentive to needs and intent on supporting development, leaders need to provide an environment through relational approaches where enough challenge is provided to help stretch and develop those they are leading but without this feeling unsafe and overwhelming. It is an intricate balance to manage not least because of the volatility that surrounds contemporary health and social care practice. The challenge therefore is how to achieve a stable relationship without resorting to denial of the unpredictable (Cardona, 2020). In taking a reality-based approach that does not deny the complexity and difficulties inherent in providing high-quality health and social care, gives the leader and organisation, the opportunity to effectively engage in the experiences of what it is to provide and receive care within this context.

As such, leaders and an organisational culture that can identify with some of the projections from clients, and we would say staff as well, means there is more likelihood of being in touch with core issues of task. The capacity to listen to one's own experience and hear the message from others is a fundamental tool to understand (Cardona, 2020). This in turn has the potential for staff to experience their leaders as attuned to their experiences and engaged with those around them, as opposed to being distant and remote.

Primary tasks and leaders

Good leadership is about helping followers to face anxiety (Alford, 2001) support of team members is core, or as will be explained here, one of the primary tasks of leaders. The primary task is the task an organisation must perform if it is to survive (Rice, 1963). Health and social care cannot be effective without supporting those who are delivering it, an understanding of the primary tasks of an organisation, and we can always argue there is more than one, is a way of keeping on track and a reference point when there is deviation. Analysis of the primary task can highlight discrepancies between what an organization sets out to do and what is happening; this helps to clarify and understand activities, roles and experiences of individuals in relation to each other and the organisation as a whole (Roberts, 2009). The primary task is the task that must be addressed at that moment but must also be seen in the context of the overall strategic direction of the organization (Obholzer, 2021). This offers a way to stay on task despite competing conflicts of which there will always be many due to the complexity of health and social care.

Space to reflect

Having space to step out of the leadership role as Jon did in the mentor/mentee relationship allows a range of lenses through which to analyse one's own leadership practice. This is essential for a range of reasons including, the health of the organisation, the efficacy of the leader and the wellbeing of followers. Opening an awareness to the concepts of envy and gratitude, which otherwise would remain unconscious, in a place that is safe gives time for understanding some fundamental processes thus giving the leader the opportunity to go beyond the superficial, step away from their leader role for a safe period, and to analyse the dynamics at play.

Mentorship allows the leader to take up a different position in the relationship. We advocate that this is important in and of itself but additionally can help the leader become familiar with adopting a stance that is not just focused on their leadership role. In terms of supporting others' development, stepping up whilst the leader steps down enables learning, brings on others and is useful in succession planning (Obholzer, 2021). We acknowledge that this can be complicated, as proposed using 'Envy and Gratitude'. However, the use of reflection, discussion and mentorship as a way of enabling awareness of different perspectives, as proposed by Britton (2004), can offer support with this complicated task and enable a healthy perspective, as stressed by Obholzer (2021):

> In order to manage one's personal and organizational life, one needs to have an understanding of the processes that manifest themselves in all areas of one's life. The key is the realization that one's picture of the world and its functioning is solely one's own . . . one has, on a daily basis, to monitor not only one's own assumptions but also make allowances for the fact that any work or social intercourse requires an acknowledgement of the other perspectives.
>
> (p. 139)

Conclusion

This chapter has illustrated the use of psychodynamic approaches with a focus on leadership, followership and mentorship. This offers support to the proposal that these approaches are applicable across a range of situations and also offer depth and breadth to support consideration of the issues that are inherent in contemporary health and social care practice.

Using the reflections gathered during a mentor/mentee relationship, we have considered a challenging dynamic between a leader and team members, the essence of which we think will be familiar to many. Klein (1957) has been used to apply the concepts of envy and gratitude to the case example and in doing, we have shown how these concepts, controversy aside, can be applied to help open perspectives on perplexing situations which at first seem difficult to make sense of.

The discussion has held the central themes of formative caregiver relationships as the foundation on which all subsequent relationships are built. This includes professional relationships as illustrated between Jon, Simon, Paula and the mentor. Holding in mind the concepts of object relations can offer a framework to consider what is being provided and conversely neglected within the dynamic. We also stressed the importance of holding a position which allows self-observation and monitoring. This is crucial when aiming to provide a supportive, containing environment to the world of work.

References

Alford, C.F. (2001) Leadership by Interpretation and Holding. *Organisational and Social Dynamics*, (2), 153–173.

Bateman, A., & Holmes, J. (2008) *Introduction to Psychoanalysis Contemporary Theory and Practice*. London & New York. Routledge.

Bion, W.R. (1962) *Learning from Experience*. London. Heinemann.

Bott Spillius, E., Milton, J., Garvey, P., Couve, C, & Steiner, D. (2011) *The New Dictionary of Kleinian Thought*. London & New York. Routledge Taylor & Francis Group.

Britton, R. (2004) *Sex, Death, and the Superego Experiences in Psychoanalysis*. London & New York. Karnac.

Cardona, F. (2020) *Work Matters Consulting to Leader Sand Organizations in the Tavistock Tradition*. London & New York. Routledge Taylor & Francis Group.

Klein, M. (1957) *Envy and Gratitude and Other Works 1946–1963*. London. Vintage.

Likierman, M. (2015) *Melanie Klein: Her Work in Context*. London. Bloomsbury Publishing Plc.

Obholzer, A. (2021) *Workplace Intelligence Unconscious Forces and How to Manage Them*. London & New York. Routledge Taylor & Francis group.

Rice, A.K. (1963) *The Enterprise and its Environment*. London. Tavistock Publications.

Roberts, V.Z. (2009) The organization of work: Contributions from open systems theory in Obholzer, O., & Roberts, V.Z. (eds) *The Unconscious at Work Individual and Organizational Stress in the Human Services*. London & New York. Routledge Taylor Francis Group.

Roth, P. (2008) Introduction in Roth, P., & Lemma, A. (eds) *Envy and Gratitude Revisited*. London & New York. Routledge Taylor Francis Group.

Winnicott, D. W. (1953) Transitional Objects and Transitional Phenomena – a Study of the First Not-Me Possession. *International Journal of Psycho-Analysis*, 34, 89, 9p.

Chapter 7

How 'Our Adult World and Its Roots in Infancy' (Klein, 1959), affects our abilities to make use of contemporary health and social care services

Celeste Foster

Introduction

The aim of this chapter is to outline how taking a developmental perspective to the understanding of staff and service user experiences, and responses within the professional-service-user relationship, can improve care outcomes. Developing an increased awareness of how experiential learning from our most formative relationships in early life continues to be encoded in our responses to others in adulthood and often reactivated in everyday encounters in health and social care settings can help us stay on task, improve connections with those we care for and recognise the need for our own support.

The psychoanalytic developmental object relations theories of Melanie Klein, and those who followed her (e.g. Segal, Winnicott and Bion), are not only theories and techniques to guide psychotherapists on how to intervene in cases where there is psychological disturbance. They are theories of our human development: of how all of us come to be who we are, the essential role that our formative relationships and experiences in early life have in shaping that process and the ways in which our early experiences continue to influence us across the life course. Never is this more important to consider than when thinking about how we relate to helping institutions and professionals in the face of ill health.

In the last 20 years, the advent of adverse childhood experience (ACE) research has influenced our understanding of mental and physical health problems, combined with increasing understanding of the importance of adopting trauma-informed care in health and social care settings. In this context, it might be possible to wonder what a mid-20th-century object relations theory, with its array of unusual and slightly antiquated terms (introjection, phantasy with a 'ph', and persecutory anxiety) has left to contribute to contemporary health and social care?

However, the enduring contribution of Klein's work, summarised in her seminal paper 'The Adult World and Its Roots in Infancy', is an ontological understanding that it is not just the traumatised and hurt who see the social world through glasses made of every experience that has gone before them and who bring powerful unresolved emotional remnants of their early life to the table in any relational encounter. It is all of us, whichever side of the professional–service user/patient/

DOI: 10.4324/9781003541660-8

client relationship we are on, in all of our everyday emotional and relational management tasks and in ways that can be both helpful and actively unhelpful (Klein, 1959). In addition, by focusing on the quality of the emotional dynamics in our earliest relationships, including the relationship between the external world and the version of this world that builds up inside our own mind, Klein produced a means of understanding the specific and nuanced characteristics of relational challenges for individuals. This understanding goes beyond a general principle that unfavourable circumstances can produce emotional and relational challenges in adulthood, making it available for application in practice day to day.

Engaging with bodies that are not working as they should, or as we hoped, and with the health and/or social care services and professionals employed to help us, brings us in to touch with our more childlike feelings – vulnerability, anxiety and dependency. The re-emergence of a body that cannot do everything for itself takes us back, often in ways outside of our conscious awareness, to the complex experiences and patterns unique to our particular infancy and childhood, when we were reliant upon others for our survival (Klein, 1937). As health problems threaten our bodies, and the minds housed within them, they bring us not just into contact with how we feel about our own bodies but also the people who gave us our bodies and the health and social care practitioners who come to symbolise those original caregivers. As Klein (1959) highlights, even the very best early care circumstances stir up both loving and destructive feelings, as the experience of utter dependency on an all-knowing, all-powerful carer can't help but produce fear, frustration, resentment and at times rage.

In her observations during her own recovery from surgery, Klein (1937) conceptualised the experience of being ill or in recovery as a return to the earliest pre-verbal anxiety and danger situations experienced in infancy. To put it another way, the experience of needing help and being helped can at best feel like a temporary threat to one's sense of self-integrity. In cases where difficult early experiences have left us with untended wounds, it can feel like the 'trauma of being the victim of . . . help' (Tarachow, 1963, p. 49).

In a parallel process, the experience for professionals of having their attempts at help rejected, denigrated and dismissed can equally reactivate their early patterns of relating to others. This can create a cycle of escalating distress and dysfunction, and splits between members of the patient's care team (Adshead and Guthrie, 2015). Understanding this, deepening our knowledge of the interpersonal and intrapsychic processes which may be affecting those in our care, and engaging in frank reflection on our own internal world, brings the potential to pay attention to the details of relational encounters in the workplace and consider how we can use ourselves to lessen the barriers facing our clients, no matter what our role.

Taking as an example the health care situation for a young adult managing the challenges of a long-term physical health condition alongside the ongoing transition to adult life and that of his care team, the fundamental concepts contained in Klein's theory of the development will be laid out and applied to the patient–professional–team triad, for the purpose of increasing understanding of the implications for people working in all kinds of helping roles in everyday health and social care practice.

The reader will be encouraged to reflect on their own experiences and invited to understand the importance of working to set the relational conditions, wherever possible, for professional therapeutic relationships that do not inadvertently replicate disturbing aspects of the client's life experiences. Practitioner sensitivity to the potential for hidden but powerful feelings associated with infancy and childhood to emerge in patient–professional relationships can offer the chance for re-working such experiences through everyday exchange to support clients to be able to take in and make use of the health care provision they are being offered. The importance of supported space for both patient and professionals to provide opportunity for reflection and self-care will be emphasised.

Case example

For the purpose of preserving confidentiality, the case example has been written inspired by composite and disguised material from a number of cases and experiences in the author's clinical work (Winship et al., 2024). No individual family is represented in the case material.

Toby is a 21-year-old man with a diagnosis of systemic lupus erythematosus (SLE) who receives treatment in a multiprofessional outpatient clinic. His symptoms include muscle and joint pain, fatigue and chronic headaches. He was under the care of a paediatric team from his diagnosis at 16 years until he was transferred over to the adult service before his 19th birthday. Toby's illness impacted his educational achievements, and he has not been able to find a job that he can maintain due to his symptoms. He lives at home with his mum. Toby is dependent on his mum to help get to appointments and manage picking up his prescriptions. He is often observed speaking to his mum in the waiting room in an irritated and disparaging way.

Toby's parents separated when he was approximately five years old. His father lives in the local area, but Toby does not have contact with him. As part of his initial assessment for the clinic, Toby disclosed that his mum and dad's relationship was characterised by domestic violence perpetrated by his dad. Toby remembers his dad being very angry and aggressive and being frightened of him. Toby's mum is registered disabled; the notes from the paediatric clinic suggest that her injuries and health needs are related to her experience of domestic violence.

Toby is seen in clinic by a medical consultant and a lupus specialist nurse. He has declined appointments with occupational therapy or psychology. Members of the team are split between those who are very worried about him and those who feel he does not want to help himself and is wasting their time. Toby struggles to adhere to self-management advice. He often turns up late for appointments or attends the clinic needing urgent help when he has no planned appointment, causing a scene in the reception area in front of other patients if he is not seen quickly.

His relationship with the consultant is strained. He does not take his medicines as prescribed; he often tells the consultant that he doesn't trust that she knows what she is doing and that only he knows how to take the medicines to best effect. Toby can respond to expressions of care by stating that his condition 'doesn't bother me, I'm used to it' but equally experiences changes in prescribed medicines as punishment, which can provoke very angry, disparaging responses. At these times, the consultant can get drawn into arguments with him, and appointments can end with him in tears pleading for more medicine.

The consultant has confided in the psychologist that she dreads appointments with Toby and wants to discharge him as soon as possible. Conversely, the specialist nurse is very worried about Toby's vulnerability. She appears to have a much better relationship with Toby; in fact Toby often tells the consultant that the nurse is the only person who really listens to him. The nurse often tries to accommodate Toby's requests for flexible, ad hoc appointments and with home visits, but on busy clinic days, she can fall short of the promises she makes, keeping him waiting.

Toby recently attended the clinic and was seen berating the nurse, shouting and squaring up to her in the clinic room, due to home visit cancellation at short notice. At the next team meeting, the consultant suggests that he be discharged on the basis of the clinic's zero tolerance policy to aggression and disrespectful behaviour. The nurse advocates for giving Toby another chance.

Overview of the paper

Klein's essay 'Our Adult World and Its Roots in Infancy', was written for a non-psychoanalytically trained audience. Published in 1959, it condenses all of her well-known theories from 1922 to that date, into an integrated and accessible account of how our sense of self, mental life, relatedness to others and understanding of the world are socially constructed from birth onwards. Therefore, it is not an easy task to precis the key elements in non-technical form, as the paper is in effect Klein's own plain English summary of her grand theory of development across the life course.

Klein was a psychoanalyst who worked predominantly with children. Unlike Freud, whose theories of psychological development in childhood and early life were traced back and extrapolated from the insights he gained in his analysis of adults, Klein prospectively tracked in detail the development of mental life through infancy, childhood and beyond. She both built on and challenged Freud's work to understand and communicate the complexity of the child's emotional life. This included shining a light on the profound internal conflicts and anxieties faced in infancy and the long shadow these earliest experiences cast on the mental processes of the adult, including on our individually unique capacities for love, hate, intimacy, frustration and guilt tolerance, and reparation.

Central to understanding the theories laid out in 'Our Adult World' are the concepts of the unconscious, the ego, unconscious phantasy, primitive persecutory anxieties, internal world development and the roles of projection, introjection and splitting as instinctive mechanisms for growth and for surviving unmanageable emotions. Whilst some of these ideas were introduced in earlier chapters, they bear repeating here to build the foundations for understanding how the experience of care and its absence, or disruption, mediates intra- and interpersonal processes, driving development of the self (or personality) and our relatedness to others.

The unconscious refers to the aspect the self that falls outside of our aware-ness – our instinctive, spontaneous and unelaborated feelings, impulses, desires and responses. Klein (1959) described unconscious phantasy as the mental rep-resentations of our instinctual life representing the particular urges and feelings that dominate the mind at any given moment. For example, she hypothesised that during birth and in the post-birth period in which babies must adjust to a terrify-ing new reality and bear unpredictable moments of acute discomfort, they experi-ence overwhelming life-and-death anxiety that is of a persecutory nature. As the baby does not yet have the thinking apparatus to make sense of their experience, these overwhelming fears are felt in phantasy as though they are being inflicted upon them by a hostile external force (Klein, 1959, p. 248). Klein believed that the ego – the consciously aware and organised part of the self that works to manage the relationship with the outside world and regulate different aspects of our self – is brought into life in part by these experiences of overwhelming anxiety, developing as we instinctively try to defend ourselves from the unmanageable feelings stirred up both from outside and within.

In a situation in which the baby's needs are responded to positively (warmth, food, tenderness), the feelings of relief and soothing are felt to come from a good external force and constitute the baby's first sense of relatedness to their carer. One of Klein's (many) radical contributions to the understanding of babies was to conceive of how nuanced their emotional/instinctive experience was right from the beginning of life. She described how a baby's needs go far beyond material care and include the desire to be loved and understood – expressed and felt by the baby through the way in which their primary carers respond to and handle them, what in modern neuro-psychobiological attachment parlance we call attunement (Delaney and Ferguson, 2014).

These positive experiences of the carer are taken into (introjected) the baby's internal world as good objects and furnish our internal world with figures made up of the repeated patterns of those first significant relationships, strengthening the developing ego as it takes on some of the characteristics it internalises. In other words, the capacity to love and to relate to others is brought into being by being loved. The counterpart to introjection is projection – projecting parts of one's feel-ings and impulses outwards and into another person. Attributing one's own feeling to another and identifying with them forms the basis of a kind of early empathy (i.e. we can understand the needs of the other because they are also ours). It can also, temporarily at least, rid us of complex overwhelming feelings of hurt and anger that are unmanageable within a newly developing mind.

In Klein's model of development, it is the balance between taking in aspects of others into our inner world (introjection of objects) and expelling aspects of our own urges and feelings (projection) that is key to the particular shape that our ego and internal world develops. Taking in good objects makes it easier to take a chance on identifying with and taking in aspects of helpful others (grandparents, teachers, friends' parents), as we are primed for that experience to be repeated. If those early relationships were cold, unpredictable and destructive, then we are more likely to expect that experience again and guard ourselves against it. It also provides basis for building self-concept, as characteristics of the internalised object are acquired by the infant. In this way, we can start to see why early experiences of relationships have such a profound impact. Good experiences produce conditions for openness to more good experiences. Conversely, frightening, cold, attacking or unavailable objects furnish our internal world in a way that can close down our openness to future carer bonds and provide us with a mirror of ourselves that teaches us something very painful about who we are and what we deserve.

The relative balance of what is introjected and projected shapes up who we are and how we see the world and those in it. Too much projection and one can lose oneself in the other. If projections are predominantly hostile (e.g. anger, grievances and dissatisfaction), Klein observed that development of real empathy or capacity to consider the needs of others is disturbed. Too much introjection and the strength of one's ego is compromised as it becomes dominated by preoccupation with the other, potentially making tuning in to and privileging one's own feelings and needs more difficult. In adulthood, as we can see in the case example of Toby, we draw on our mental representations of formative childhood experiences as a basis for beliefs about whether we deserve care and whether others can be trusted to provide that care (Adshead and Guthrie, 2015). Latent unconscious phantasies related to early experiences of being vulnerable and in need can be re-activated by the experiences of physical health problems and of needing to seek help in adulthood (Barratt, 2021).

'Our Adult World' also introduces the concept of greed as it relates to development, offering a view of how both the baby's greed or neediness and the carer response to it produces complex conflict and brings instinctive coping strategies into play in order to manage. Greed can be a difficult term to think about and use in relation to babies. However, its use is important as it recognises that for actual survival and growth, a baby and the child it becomes needs to possess the capacity and freedom to be able to take in and make use of its carer's resources (e.g. milk, food, love, time) without worrying about the impact on the carer. Winnicott later referred to this as a kind of developmentally ordinary ruthlessness (Swartz, 2018).

As the primary carer represents the baby's whole world, including moments of everyday frustration, despair and pain, even the very best care circumstances means that a baby must contend with mixed feelings towards their carer. Klein (1959) renders in exquisite detail how dependency produces feelings of envy, resentment and hate as the baby must wait on their carer to make themselves available and provide that which the infant does not have but desperately needs. In turn, these aggressive feelings and impulses stir up fears of retaliation from those who are on the receiving end of their hostile feelings. Klein believed there is an innate capacity for hostile feelings and aggressive urges in all of us that varies from person to person. She also emphasised how it could be increased significantly by circumstances characterised by neglect and privation and mitigated by the provision of love, understanding and acceptance of our ordinary destructive feelings.

In circumstances that leave one feeling not good enough or loved, or where there is deprivation, ordinary feelings of greed/neediness worsen as anxiety and desperation predominate, and any satisfaction or soothing is only temporary. Klein hypothesised that the unconscious anxiety that nothing is enough also comes with insecurity about one's own capacity to love and exacerbates feelings of envy. Unresolved envy – the feeling of hatred in the moment of anyone who has something which we do not – shows up in adulthood in a range of ways from being unable to take pleasure in the successes of others (Klein, 1959) to, as we might formulate in Toby's case, rejecting or spoiling attempts to help (Bowers, 2005).

As the infant is reliant on trust in a good carer/parent, in order to be able to take in love and nourishment essential for its actual survival, Klein theorised that it must do something to keep the good/loved version of a carer (that meets its needs) and the bad/hated version (that withholds) separate. It also has to do something to defend against unmanageable aggressive impulses, and the anxieties about retaliation from the carer that they activate, which are felt to threaten the infant's existence. With the cognitive–affective apparatus to hold conflicting feelings of love, hate and fear together not yet developed, the baby experiences the good and bad aspects of the carer as separate entities. Splitting and separating of objects (good and bad) and our feelings towards them (love/hate) in this way forms the basis of one of our most instinctual coping mechanisms, which lessens over time, but even in good enough developmental circumstances is never given up entirely.

Over time, understanding that the object of our love and the object of frustration and rage are the same develops with the help of an accepting and understanding carer who can tolerate our angry attacks and not be overwhelmed by them or retaliate against us. Being helped to bear the guilt that emerges from realising that the carer you are angry with and have attacked in your mind is the same loved carer becomes a template for self-acceptance and for being able to form realistic intimate relationships in later life. It produces the understanding that people are flawed, and ability to make use of flawed helpers, friends and lovers.

This process of forming a realistic understanding of our dependency requires us to turn toward and bear painful feelings of loss, jealousy and guilt. In circumstances that support us to bear these feelings, it produces concern for the other and the wish to repair ruptures in the relationship. However, at this stage of our development, a carer who in real life is in a fragile or hurt state (Toby's mum), or one who enacts punishment on us for just being a child (Toby's dad), is a source of overwhelming stress. The child is likely to feel that they are responsible for the harms done (Bowers, 2005).

These fears of one's own destructiveness may continue well into adulthood. When the feelings feel too big to be managed, manic defences are employed to try and keep the experience of dependency at bay, through denigrating, omnipotent and contemptuous attacks on the source of our feelings of dependency as we manoeuvre inside our minds to try and feel as though we have triumphed over them and do not need them (Klein, 1946). In adulthood, splitting and manic defences may continue to be employed for the purposes of psychic survival in moments where our self/ego feels under threat rather than the actual concrete life-preserving function it served in infancy (Klein, 1959).

In this way, 'Our Adult World and Its Roots in Infancy' lays out a model of development in which the tension between care and concern for others and their malicious destruction is central to the human struggle, with love and care acting as the constraining force against more destructive impulses that result from profound existential anxiety (Alford, 1998). The raw capacity to express an instinctive caritas for the welfare of others and balance it against the meeting of one's own material and emotional survival needs is, in Klein's view, born out of an innate human capacity to identify with the suffering of others. However, it arises, or not, or in problematic ways, as a response to the specific quality of care received from one's primary carers (Klein, 1946) and the degree to which the carer's own environment enables or disturbs the process. It is reactivated and reworked in all relationships in our adult life, but particularly in those that parallel the original care relationship.

Discussion

We cannot know the exact details of Toby's object relations or the childhood, experiences that shaped them, and nor should we try to outside of the specific frame of a psychoanalysis relationship. However, Toby's case vignette does contain some pointers to their general shape that application of Klein's paper can help illuminate in order to explore the challenges faced by him and his care team and offer something about the possible direction of intervention in similar situations.

SLE is a chronic autoimmune disease of complex aetiology that affects the skin, joints, kidneys, heart and nervous system, resulting in inflammation and tissue damage. Toby developed this condition in late adolescence, and we meet him still working through the transition period of early adulthood. Toby is facing an intersectional triad of complexity: early experience of care characterised by a dynamic of violence and fear between his parents and toward him; the ordinary but nevertheless rigorous developmental challenge of late adolescence and the onset of a chronic, difficult-to-treat illness that requires engagement with multiple health professionals for effective management.

The primary tasks of late adolescence and early adulthood are developing mastery and ownership over one's body; consolidating one's identity, including occupational and psychosexual identity and independence (Waddell, 2018). As we see with Toby's ambivalent and all-or-nothing relatedness to his mum and his care team, these tasks are often disrupted by the experience of illness (Polmear, 2004). They also necessarily include working through and relinquishing dependency, which in itself can reactivate unresolved aspects of our formative relationships with caregivers.

Klein (cited in Barratt (2021) observed that when physical health conditions threaten our identity as adults, the shock to the system prompts more instinctual/primitive anxiety to reemerge as 'memories in feeling' (Klein, 1957). These have been described as 'deep, almost unreachable layers of experience which come before (and go beyond) language' (Barratt, 2021) and activate many of the same instinctual defence mechanisms we used to cope back then. Difficulties in accessing, processing and verbalising 'memory-feelings' of infant–primary carer relationships can result in the patient being again reliant on projection of unmanageable feelings into their current caregivers, including professionals (Barbasio and Granieri, 2013). Professional care providers can be on the receiving end of anxiety, neediness (greed), envy, aggression, guilt or love (Barratt, 2021).

A number of recent studies involving people experiencing chronic illnesses underpinned by autoimmune and inflammation processes have highlighted the impact of mental representations (objects) of carers and unfavourable care situations and relationships on disease onset and exacerbation and pain perception (Pinto et al., 2023; Adshead and Guthrie, 2015). In an almost exact enactment of Klein's theory, Barbasio and Granieri (2013) found that a majority of SLE participants had mental representations of unfavourable carer experiences that had left them highly unsure of their worth and dependent on affirmation from others. Yet because of their negative expectations of caregivers, they also avoided intimacy to avoid the pain of loss and rejection. They showed signs of being on-guard for any indicators that their health care providers did not like them, displayed escalating care seeking behaviour, but at the same time avoiding or finding it hard to engage fully with actual care and advice offered due to a fear of loss.

In Toby's case, we can see potential for unresolved challenges related to the period of his development described by Klein, in which normal frustration, envy and rage towards his parents as primary carers are worked through. This period will likely have been characterised by experiences of actual retaliation from an aggressive parent and moments in which destructive phantasies of attacking his mother will have been met with actual experiences of a hurt, vulnerable and frightened mum, potentially leaving him with overwhelming levels of anxiety, guilt, fears of his own capacity for aggression and an ongoing need to maintain the split between good and bad in order to survive the conflict in his own mind.

One of the particular aspects of long-term conditions such as SLE that makes such ripe ground for reactivating primitive anxieties and manic defences related to early care is that there is no 'cure'. Or, to phrase it in a different way, there is no hope of Toby freeing himself completely from some level of dependency on care providers, meaning that accessing health care has the potential to repeatedly re-trigger coping responses to earlier adverse experiences. The ongoing requirement for dependency on others for help can be particularly disturbing for young adults as they are trying to establish a sense of self-sufficiency and independence. It can produce fury towards primary caregivers, who are felt to have failed to provide them with what they needed to grow up (Dubinsky, 2004). In the case example, we can see Toby's ambivalence and frustration at feeling so reliant upon his mum, his unconscious deployment of defences that seek to reverse the experience of dependency (Bowers, 2005) through control of and contempt for health care professionals and his denial that anyone matters including himself.

Clinicians can experience this as rejection or sabotage of help, hostility or non-engagement. Being on the end of such difficult projections can erode the ability of health care practitioners to retain compassionate practice and, as we see in Toby's medical consultant, engender a wish to be rid of the patient. This is particularly so when health care practitioners are carrying their own unresolved vulnerabilities (as we all must because no one's early care experience is perfect). As Klein notes,

> When one suspects he is the object of hate all one's antisocial attitudes are increased by the feeling. . . .[But for] the person who is unable to bear criticism because it touches on one's own persecutory anxiety . . . this may even endanger the cause for which he is working.
>
> (p. 262)

Vulnerabilities in practitioners' own object relations can also be expressed through identification and collusion, not just retaliatory rejection. In the case example, the nurse's high level of worry and concern for Toby (identification) results in her bending over backwards to try and meet his needs (collusion), inadvertently providing a home for Toby's instinctual need to split his good and hateful feelings. The consultant is denigrated and hated, and the nurse is initially idealised. However, unable to fulfil her offers of flexibility and additional help, she also quickly falls from grace. As Bell (2009) notes, splitting and idealisation are always fragile and brittle defences. Inevitable error on the part of the idealized object causes the illusion to collapse leaving the patient feeling even more vulnerable, distrustful and reliant on manic defences to cope.

There is another subtle yet important point for reflection here about professional's potential unconscious bias towards service users. Patients with high levels of adherence to treatment and professional advice are often liked and encouraged by professionals as they meet our need for acceptance and to feel that we are having an impact. However, highly adherent patients are far more likely to have preoccupied rather than secure attachment styles, dominated by an anxious desire to please/appease others (Ciechanowski et al., 2004). Whilst this type of object relation pattern may feel preferable to engage with for professionals, it is often exhausting and deleterious to service users' mental health over the long term.

Implications and recommendations

Examination of 'Our Adult World' poses the question of what we are to do, especially when we are not psychotherapists, when we encounter relational difficulties with service users in everyday health and social care situations.

Ill health in adulthood and its treatment provides a re-staging of earliest experiences of dependency, which comes not just with challenge but also the opportunity of reworking to (re)gain trust in external people and one's relation to them (Klein, 1959). Having a basic understanding of the process of introjection and projection as the means of learning from and managing anxiety in relationships can help improve our responses to difficult patient encounters. Being curious about our patients' experiences beyond the symptoms/difficulties for which they are coming to us can help avoid replication of the most troubling aspects of patients' internal worlds.

Understanding that the things described in this chapter do not only happen to our patients, and that our patterns of relating and vulnerabilities derived from the imperfect nature of our early care experiences are also at play, is key. Developing increased self-awareness of how internal relations and experiences impact our approach, particularly when we feel under attack from patients, can go a very long way to lessening conflict and setting the conditions in which a patient can accept and take in the help that is offered. In this way we can all contribute to helping those who fear that they are unworthy, and that others are withholding and retaliatory, to better access the health care they need and deserve. As Adshead and Guthrie (2015) highlight, problems in professional caring relationships go both ways. Feelings of frustration and resentment towards patients who do not adhere to advice and who appear not to care, or to want to get better, have a direct negative impact on care outcomes (Sloan et al., 2020).

Reflecting on our own motivations for how we relate to individual patients requires space, and often the help of others. In the case example, talking as a team sharing experiences of how it felt to be in Toby's company, not just clinical case management discussions, may have been helpful. Whilst it can feel uncomfortable, owning up to unspoken negative feelings towards a patient can actually reduce the chances of them being acted out in difficult encounters with them (Alvarez, 2012). Talking openly with peers can also help to see the potential splits developing and agreeing on a more coordinated way forwards, as well as providing peer support with the feelings of being under attack or under continuous pressure to accommodate demands.

Even with space to reflect, keeping our cool when envy, greed and grievances relating to feelings of deprivation are at the fore of a patient's communications can be easier said than done, but there are some principles from Klein's paper that can be applied. Avoiding the impulse to collude (give in to unrealistic demands), deny the relational difficulties or respond with condemnation and outrage are important first steps (Alvarez, 2012). These reflexive ways of managing are understandable when under pressure but tend only to heighten the patient's anxiety, and inadvertently reinforce reliance on primitive defences.

Proactive provision of information about expectations, boundaries, and what can realistically be offered by yourself and the service for which you work, can create relational security (Sloan et al., 2020). Attunement – listening hard, noticing and naming direct and indirectly expressed needs and responding to them practically and without judgement – can soothe anxiety. For example, being on the end of accusations of being useless may reflect a person's experience of them having a 'useless body', of us being unable to cure their condition, and the activation of early painful experiences of a carer who could not meet their needs. Being able to acknowledge and accept the disappointment, hurt and anger that the patient feels

without feeling personally responsible can provide opportunity to reflect on experience and the introjection/projection dynamic of a new experience (Alvarez, 2012).

Making choice, autonomy and collaboration explicit from the outset can
help people who may have had to be very self-sufficient or experienced profound helplessness in face of awful experiences. Involving patients as part of the
decision-making team and enabling them to come to their own understanding and
formulate their own plans of care can mitigate anxiety stirred by dependency, support empowerment and improve outcomes (Lemma, 2024; Sloan et al., 2020).

Conclusion

In this chapter, I have presented an application of Klein's (1959) paper 'Our Adult
World and Its Roots in Infancy' to the challenges that can arise in professional–
service user relationships when people seek intervention for health difficulties. It
provides a dynamic framework for understanding how the development of mental
functioning and a sense of one's identity and subjectivity in adulthood unfolds
through intimate relationships with carers starting at birth, and probably before,
and continue to be shaped, reactivated and reworked through relational experiences
throughout the life course. The concept of childhood trauma, with a big T, is now
well understood and often relatively easy to see in people we care for. However, the
impacts of small moment-to-moment details of emotional and relational difficulty
repeated over time can be much harder to notice.

Klein's model of object relations, and at its heart an internal world that is
slowly built up from repetition of everyday relational encounters, can help us take
a more compassionate view of all of our patients and help to sustain our professional optimism in even the most complex or difficult of cases. Just as in infancy,
capacities for self-care and recovery often develop in adults facing physical health
challenges from the repetition of tiny details of moment-to-moment care in the
here and now and depend on the professional carer taking time to understand their
own responses, not just those of their patients. Forging relationships that provide
a safe, reliable experience of being cared for furnishes people's hearts and minds
with skills that will help them heal their own wounds, fanning the embers of hope
and belief in their own value. People can hold these experiences in mind long after
the relationship they have with us, priming them for more good experiences in the
future (Foster, 2020).

References

Adshead, G., & Guthrie, E. (2015). The role of attachment in medically unexplained symptoms and long term illness. *British Journal of Psychiatric Advances*, 21, 167–174.
Alford, C. F. (1998). Melanie Klein and the nature of good and evil. In: Marcus, P., & Rosen-
burg, A. (Eds.), *Psychoanalytic versions of the human condition: Philosophies of life and
their impact on practice* (118–139). New York: New York University Press.
Alvarez, A. (2012). *The thinking heart: Three levels of psychoanalytic therapy with disturbed children*. Routledge.

Barbasio, C., & Granieri, A. (2013). Emotion regulation and mental representation of attachment in patients with systemic lupus erythematosus: A study using the Adult Attachment Interview. *The Journal of Nervous and Mental Disease*, 201(4), 304–310.

Barratt, H. (2021). 'Strong clinging to objects': Materiality and relationality in Melanie Klein's Observations after an Operation. (1937). *Wellcome Open Research*, 6, 40. https://wellcomeopenresearch.org/articles/6-40/v1

Bell, D. (2009). Projective identification. In: Bronstein, C. (Ed.), *Kleinian theory: A contemporary perspective*. Wiley & Sons.

Bower, M. (2005). Working with families who see help as the problem. In: Bower, M. (Ed.), *Psychoanalytic theory for social work practice: Thinking under fire*. London: Routledge.

Ciechanowski, P., Russo, J., Katon, W., Von Korff, M., Ludman, E., Lin, E., . . . Bush, T. (2004). Influence of patient attachment style on self-care and outcomes in diabetes. *Psychosomatic Medicine*, 66(5), 720–728.

Delaney, K., & Ferguson, J. (2014). Peplau and the brain: Why interpersonal neuroscience provides a useful language for the relationship process. *Journal of Nursing Education and Practice*, 4(8), 145–152.

Dubinsky, H. (2004). *Brief psychotherapy with adolescents*. London: Tavistock Clinic Series, Karnac.

Foster, C. (2020). Evaluating the impact of a psychodynamic work discussion group for mental health nurses in Adolescent PICU. *Archives of Psychiatric Nursing*, 34(6), 481–491. https://doi.org/10.1016/j.apnu.2020.08.008

Klein, M. (1937). *Observations after an operation. Wellcome Library* (Klein: Unpublished Papers, PP/KLE/C.95). London.

Klein, M. (1946 [1988]). Notes on some schizoid mechanisms. In: Kein, M. (Ed.), *Envy & gratitude and other works, 1946–63*. London: Virago.

Klein, M. (1957 [1988]). Envy and gratitude. In: Klein, M. (Ed.), *Envy & gratitude and other works, 1946–63*. London: Virago.

Klein, M. (1959 [1975]). Our adult world and its roots in infancy. In: Klein, M. (Ed.), *Envy and Gratitude and Other Works 1946–1963*. Edited by: Masud, M., & Khan, R. London: The Hogarth Press.

Lemma, A. (2024). *Introduction to the practice of psychoanalytic psychotherapy*. 3rd Edition. John Wiley and Sons.

Pinto, A. M., Luís, M., Geenen, R., Palavra, F., Lumley, M. A., Ablin, J. N., . . . da Silva, J. A. (2023). Neurophysiological and psychosocial mechanisms of fibromyalgia: A comprehensive review and call for an integrative model. *Neuroscience & Biobehavioral Reviews*, 151, 105235.

Polmear, C. (2004). Dying to live: Mourning, melancholia and the adolescent process. *Journal of Child Psychotherapy*, 30(3), 263–274.

Sloan, M., Naughton, F., Harwood, R., Lever, E., D' Cruz, D., Sutton, S., . . . Gordon, C. (2020). Is it me? The impact of patient–physician interactions on lupus patients' psychological well-being, cognition and health-care-seeking behaviour. *Rheumatology Advances in Practice*, 4(2), rkaa037.

Swartz, S. (2018). *Ruthless Winnicott: The role of ruthlessness in psychoanalysis and political protest*. Routledge.

Tarachow, S. (1963). *In introduction to psychotherapy*. New York: International University Press.

Waddell, M. (2018). *On adolescence: Inside stories*. Routledge.

Winship, G., Scott, A., & Edgar, J. (2024). Towards a psychotherapy publishing ethics concordat. *European Journal of Psychotherapy & Counselling*, 26(3–4), 411–427. https://doi.org/10.1080/13642537.2024.2384864.

Chapter 8

Bion's (1962) 'A Psycho-Analytic Study of Thinking'

Understanding how the mind of the other produces and sustains the capacity to 'think under emotional fire' for young people and staff within residential care environments

Celeste Foster

Introduction

The aim of this chapter is to provide elaboration of Bion's (1962a) 'The Psycho-Analytic Study of Thinking' and highlight its utility for guiding everyday care provision in residential social and mental health care settings. Bion's philosophical model places emotional experience at the core of understanding how mental functioning first emerges in early life and centres unequivocally the need for emotionally receptive and thoughtful carers to be available to us in order for us to develop the capacities to recognise, tolerate, manage and think about intense emotional states. Termed alpha function by Bion and often referred to in contemporary applications of his work as mentalisation, Yakeley describes alpha function/mentalisation as

> the capacity to reflect and understand the contents and processes of our own and other people's mental states, including thoughts, beliefs, desires, affects, wishes, and intentions, and to be able to interpret our own actions and those of others as meaningful, and based on intentional mental states.
>
> (2018, p. 6)

These capacities are now well understood as emerging from within the intersubjective relationship between child and caregiver, and to be implicated in both mental wellbeing and distress across the life course.

Bion's paper offers a dynamic model and framework for understanding the specific qualities and relational processes associated with the kind of growth-promoting, emotionally containing relationship that brings this aspect of consciousness into life; what can happen when the process goes awry and how the same qualities needed in the original infant–carer situation can provide therapeutic and reparatory value for individuals struggling with unmanageable emotional states in any stage of life.

DOI: 10.4324/9781003541660-9

Bion's contribution to understanding the emergence of mental life in infancy and childhood developed from his work with people with significant psychological disturbance and complex mental health needs, often related to traumatic experience or fundamental disruptions in early care experiences (Bion, 1957, 1958). He observed that in such circumstances, the traditional tool of psychoanalysis – providing interpretations of the patient's unconsciously communicated material – was not just unhelpful but actively disorganising and distressing to patients, requiring the therapist to do something else to help (Brown, 2012). Bion formulated that the task in such cases was for the worker to be open to taking in the disturbing raw emotions being projected by the patient and to bear the stress and strain of tolerating and feeling these projections rather than seeking to get rid of them though verbal analysis (Bion, 1959; Brown, 2012).

Using an example from the care of young people in a residential children's home environment, with this chapter I seek to illustrate how application of the key concepts from within 'The Psycho-Analytic Study of Thinking' (Bion, 1962a) can help to shine a light on the invisible therapeutic tasks involved in everyday care provision that are needed to promote recovery from complex mental health needs for young people whose developmental trajectory has been significantly disrupted. The utility of Bion's theory of thinking to help care staff increase awareness of the emotional impact of such work upon them, and use this awareness to care for both young people and themselves, is also emphasised. A case is made for the ongoing support needs of residential care staff to maintain their own capacity to think in the pressured and emotionally 'hot' circumstances that being in close physical and relational proximity with young people who have had fundamental ruptures in their early care experience produces.

Bion's paper contains many conceptual contributions to a more comprehensive model of how the thinking process emerges in infancy and continues to be shaped by relational experiences throughout the life course, which he developed further in his subsequent work 'Learning From Experience' (Bion, 1962b). For the purposes of this chapter, the focus will be on application of five interrelated concepts and their implications for contemporary care settings:

- The emergence of thoughts in response to the baby's raw experience of itself and the world around it and the unbearable emotions that can be associated with such thoughts.
- The role of the mind of the other (alpha function) in supporting tolerance of such unmanageable emotions and development of the baby's own alpha function.
- The characteristics of the container–contained relationship, including the capacity for reverie.
- The role of projective identification in providing an essential preverbal communication link between infant and carer within the container–contained relationship.
- What happens when there is failure in the ordinary process of projective identification.

The value of Bion's theory in the particular context set out is three-fold. It underlines the ways in which emotional experience can drive growth of thinking and at the same time how too much intensity of emotionality, without help from another, forecloses or disturbs the ability to manage and think about one's own emotional states. It reminds us of the therapeutic power of taking a thoughtful and receptive position to service users verbal and non-verbal communication (Bower, 2005), and importantly, that the task of being an available container for clients is often disturbing and can in itself make the business of thinking exceptionally hard and prone to disruption.

Case example

For the purpose of preserving confidentiality, the case example has been written using composite material from a number of cases and experiences in the author's clinical work (Winship et al., 2024). No individual, family or children's home is represented in the case material.

Maple view is an intensive residential setting for young people aged 14 to 18 years. Up to five young people live there, with 24-hour care provided by residential social workers and care assistants. All the young people in the setting are care-experienced or care-leavers and have complex mental health needs related to experiencing complex developmental trauma. In individual ways, each resident struggles with emotional and cognitive regulation, disturbance of self-concept, behavioural/impulse control and self-harm (Cook et al., 2005). The home uses an attachment-informed approach to care that also seeks to support the young people's increasing move towards independence. Intensive intermittent observations are used as standard practice (10-minute intervals) and woven into a framework of creating predictable relationships with a small team of staff, inviting all young people into everyday social interactions and independent living activities within the home and supporting them to meet their individualised therapeutic timetables.

The staff have weekly reflective practice meetings facilitated by a psychotherapist. In one of these groups, staff bring a young person recently admitted whose difficulties and how to manage them have produced disagreement between team members. Colby, 17 years of age, has a childhood history of extensive neglect and deprivation. They have recently been discharged from a mental health inpatient hospital where they received treatment for a major depressive episode. At the beginning of the meeting, the group express what seems to be a universally shared and emphatic wish for Colby to be moved on from the house due to believing that she is not appropriate for the service and is a bad influence on the other young people.

Since arriving at Maple View, Colby has struggled to engage with the therapeutic activities on offer and has tended to avoid interaction with other young people. She does not like being alone in her room, preferring to spend time in the common areas. Colby has been having what they describe as panic attacks. Staff report feeling confused about the nature of these episodes and in the meeting share differences of opinion about the underlying causes. All staff agree that it tends to start with Colby developing a pensive or 'checked-out' expression and note it becomes more difficult to engage her in conversation. She often begins to shake and pace and look physically tense. Some staff think she looks frightened at these times, whilst other's view is that she looks angry.

In these moments, Colby is prone to outbursts of explosive verbal and physical aggression, destruction to property and threats of violence. Other young people and some staff have reported feeling very frightened by these episodes and other staff describe the feeling of being on 'pins' throughout the shift for fear of what will happen. After the episodes, especially when Colby has been physically aggressive, she can deny her actions, say she doesn't remember and doesn't want to talk about it or place the blame on particular staff members.

Feelings in the staff group are running high. Some staff members observe that the episodes do not always seem worry related and so are struggling to believe that they are panic attacks. They report feeling played, as though the young person might not be being honest with them and in more control than they are letting on. Other staff feel a great deal of worry for Colby and feel that she is very vulnerable, struggling to cope with the degree of sadness and hopelessness they feel when they spend time with her, admitting to a feeling of dread when they are allocated to her care. Other staff describe feeling worn out and angry toward Colby, and angry on behalf of the other four young people whose home environment they feel is being disturbed. These differences in staff experiences play out in how Colby's needs are being managed. Some staff are taking a more authoritarian parental approach, and some seek to placate and appease Colby for fear of there being an incident. Some report noticing that they are either avoiding spending time in her company and/or breaking their own 'rules' in terms of how much lee-way they give, or how far they are prepared to bend house rules due to feeling bad for her.

All staff agree that they feel confounded as a team and find the experience of caring for Colby overwhelming. Such is their worry that in a rare move for the team, they have temporarily increased her observation levels to 1:1 continuous observations, to try and reduce the risks and see if they can intervene earlier to avoid episodes happening. In the week since the 1:1 observations have been implemented Colby's level of verbal aggression and intimidation towards staff seems to have increased, and she has begun rubbing her face repeatedly on the carpet producing friction burns. Some staff have felt compelled to intervene to try and stop this, whilst others report feeling shocked, angry and helpless in the face of this new behaviour.

Overview of the paper

Bion's (1962a) paper, the psychoanalytic study of thinking, is exactly as it says on the tin. It lays out a detailed conceptualisation of how from being born into the world as a primarily instinctual and sensory (not cognitive) being, the availability or not of another's mind and care provides the relational machinery with which to build our own mind, a mind in which affective perceptions and emotionally laden thoughts can be housed, experienced, ascribed meaning, thought about, transformed and worked with to build ever more complex understanding of ourselves and the external world.

Central to understanding Bion's paper is understanding some key assumptions built into his model. Bion hypothesised that development of thoughts came before the capacity for thinking, which he proposed is the apparatus for coping with and thinking about thoughts. Thoughts are understood to be derived from raw emotional experiences that are unmanageable for the baby, for example the experience of there being no breast or milk available to satisfy the instinctual awareness of wanting food and succour. Anyone who has been in proximity to a newborn when it is hungry knows firsthand just how temporarily catastrophic waiting for a bottle to be cooled, or to be helped to latch on to their mother's breast can be.

The capacity for thinking (adding psychological meaning to one's experience) in Bion's theory develops in order to cope with the rudimentary thoughts or conscious awareness of the distressing affect that accompany these overwhelming moments (Ogden, 2008). But that thinking is dependent on someone else being able to help soothe the distress and frustration and make sense of your experience for you. Whilst models of childcare vary significantly around the world and between cultures and families, there is fair consensus that a baby's cry contains meaning: that they are telling us something important even if they don't know what that meaning is and that it must be someone's job to try and soothe the baby's distress whilst working out what the cry means so they can respond to it helpfully. The repeated experience of this within an infant–carer relationship is what Bion (1962a) coined the 'container–contained relationship', sometimes referred to as emotional containment.

However difficult the reality of bearing a baby's cry and raw emotion held within it, most people recognise in theory at least that the baby knows something is wrong or needed but is helpless to understand and meet its own needs in that moment, alongside the need to lend one's own psychological, emotional and physical resources to the baby to help them out of the state that they are in.

In good enough circumstances, this process is characterised by the carer's capacity to notice, take in, tolerate and make sense of the infant's non-verbal communications (good and bad). It can be thought of as lending one's brain and thinking power to the child, what Bion (1962a) termed alpha function. In attachment theory terms, it is the capacity of the carer to be attuned and responsive, accepting of all aspects of the baby. This acceptance and understanding is communicated by the carer through the way in which the baby is handled and held within the carer's gaze (Winnicott, 1971) and within the intersubjective space between carer and baby via tactile and gestural cues of the body (Schore and Schore, 2014). These repeated interactional processes govern both the infant's experience of anxiety and the development of their cognitive, emotional and interpersonal functioning, resilience and understanding of themselves. This includes their relation to the world around them and the figures it is peopled by (Reisenberg-Malcom, 2001).

Bion's paper is particularly concerned about elaborating the invisible mental processes at play, rather than the slightly easier to observe attachment/holding' behaviours. Whilst it might sound a bit clunky compared to the term emotional containment, "container–contained relationship" draws attention to Bion's conceptual contribution that both the baby and the carer play an active part in the process. Carer and baby are two halves of an iterative sensory–affective–cognitive thinking machine. For the baby's part, it has to somehow make its bodily felt, not yet understood, affective experience (what Bion described as raw sense-data) available to its carer in some way.

Building on Klein's (1959 [1975]) conceptualisation of projective identification, Bion extended understanding of the term beyond an instinctual mechanism for ridding ourselves of unbearable emotional states by ascribing it to another, to what he called ordinary or realistic projective identification. This is our first means of communication and essential to our survival in creating an emotional link to our carers, joining the two parts of the thinking machine. It is an innate ability to stir up feelings in our carers through non-verbal processes to both communicate and get rid of raw unmanageable states of being in order to enlist our carer's help to soothe us and to make our experiences available to them for decoding and detoxifying, in order to have our needs met.

Bion coined the term 'reverie' to describe the aspect of the carer's alpha function, which transforms the baby's raw sensory perception data/affective experience into meaningful emotional experience/conscious awareness or thoughts that the baby can then take back in as part of its own developing mind. It requires receptivity to projected emotional states through all aspects of the child's direct and indirect communications, including those that feel hostile. Secondly, it requires the ability to tolerate the stress associated with really taking them in, feeling something of them and thinking about them in order to make them understandable without being overwhelmed (Waddell, 2007). Thirdly, it requires the ability to put the understanding into a helpful form that baby can take in and make use of as part of its own developing mind.

Derived from the French word 'to dream', reverie describes the process by which carers work to bring the baby's mind and its awareness of what is going on inside itself into life. We work to feel our way into the baby's place using our own knowledge and life experience to imagine or dream up, what might be going on for them and then respond to them in a way that they can take back in (a bottle, or breast, for a hungry baby for example) so that as well as being soothed the baby can learn something about itself from the experience ('I am hungry!').

Although the processes of the container–contained relationship are often described in terms of the parent–infant relationship, they continue to operate throughout all stages of development. In good enough circumstances, the reliance on projective identification is increasingly replaced by language as we get older and we are helped to attach names and meaning to felt experience. However, it is never completely gotten rid of and is often returned to during times of stress. In particular, adolescence has been identified as a developmental period in which there is a return to reliance on this mechanism of communicating due to the mismatch between the intensity of the emotions being experienced by young people and their not yet fully developed language (Briggs, 2009).

As a child moves into adolescence, the task of emotional containment becomes the function not just of its immediate carers but of its wider community and adults who people the systems and organisations in which they live and learn (Waddell, 2018). Bion's contribution to work with psychologically distressed patients and service users of all ages was to understand that the process of emotional containment and specifically the provision of reverie should be at the heart of all interventions that enable therapeutic change and recovery (Riesenberg-Malcolm, 2001), particularly in cases where something went wrong in the original experiences of the container–contained relationship in childhood.

In situations where there is not an available carer who is receptive to our need to have our felt experiences contained and understood, Bion hypothesised that the experience was much worse than just absence. The infant is understood in this model of thinking as experiencing the lack of availability as a kind of psychic abandonment (Brown, 2012). They are left with no option but to take back in their projected raw affective experience in its still un-understandable but emotionally intensified form, felt as a 'nameless dread', and with it their learning about the other, which is internalised as a 'wilfully misunderstanding object' (Bion, 1962a).

Transient and intermittent experiences of this kind are not likely to present long-lasting difficulties and may even in some circumstances drive growth of frustration tolerance when the baby is not left in this state for too long. However, repeated experiences are understood to be highly deleterious to the child's emotional and mental development. Left with frightening intensified emotional states that are more than they have the capacity to bear results in infants having to develop their own instinctive ways of coping, through avoidance and denial (un-thinking), modification or trivialisation of the experience for the function of reducing awareness of its painful nature or increased intensity of attempts to expel unmanageable feelings through excessive use of projective identification (Brown, 2012; Bion, 1962a).

Discussion

The provision of emotional containment and specifically reverie should be an almost continuous process in the care of mentally distressed people (Riesenberg-Malcolm, 2001). But as we can see within the case example, whilst the principles of being receptive and thoughtful can be easy to explain and appear an obvious given, the realities of actually providing it for young people such as Colby whose original experiences were lacking or disrupted is incredibly difficult. Bion (1962a) noted that as reverie is essential to development, people who lacked emotional containment as children will project with great intensity when the possibility arises, no matter their age. This is manifest in how the increased observation and therefore proximity of carers resulted in Colby literally wearing her unmanageable pain on her face, stirring a range of equally distressing feelings in the staff undertaking her 1:1 observations.

Bion's work reminds us that to some extent, workers feeling assaulted by disturbing feelings is both an inevitable and predictable component of care work. Further, the process of being able to bear the destructive and hostile parts of young people without being permanently hurt or overwhelmed by them or being pushed into reacting in critical or punitive ways – no matter how arousing the young person's behaviour might be – should be seen as a core task even though it is essentially invisible until it goes wrong. Contemporary neuropsychological studies have shown how emotional distress and dysregulated affect are rapidly communicated through unconscious body-based intersubjective communications before words can be found for them (Schore and Schore, 2014). As such, the ability to track verbal and non-verbal moment-to-moment fluctuations/rhythms in young people's internal states and to continuously modify one's own behaviour and responses, in order to be in synchrony with these, has been asserted as the foundation of effective therapeutic relationships (Schore and Schore, 2010). Despite this, attention is rarely given within organisations to the ongoing emotional toll of this more invisible element of care work (Weightman and Smithson, 2020).

A study investigating the work of nurses in inpatient mental health wards for young people found that staff came to know and understand the young people in their care primarily through the way in which the young people made them feel (Foster and Smedley, 2019a). Acting as a collective emotional container and sense maker for the indirectly transmitted emotional components of the young people's communication (projective identification) was found to be the team's most effective tool for intervening to reduce distress, and over time for helping young people to recognise and name feelings rather than acting them out. The nascent emotional and cognitive development of adolescents means that workers are required to create relational conditions in which young people can show rather than tell their story through their behaviour within care relationships with adults who are prepared to feel something of the story, not just see it; in order for them to translate it into words or helpful actions. This process requires staff to withstand and make sense of a high level of intrusion and violence disinhibition as a primary means by which distressed young people communicate and rid themselves of unmanageable pain and vulnerability.

Whilst reverie is the taking in and digesting an other's experiences, it is not a merger of the child's and the carer's feelings. It requires lending one's own apparatus in the service of the other whilst all the time recognising the other's separateness and seeing one's own position on that which is taken in and digested (Bion, 1962a). Being in proximity to young people's projected disturbance for extended periods of time can make this very hard. As we can see in the case example, staff can become concretely identified with the young person's experience of neglect, or with the aggressor, leading to persecutory and anxious appraisals of young people and colleagues and employment of some of the same unconscious defence mechanisms used by the young people, namely, splitting, projection and attempts to control the environment and get rid of unmanageable states of mind represented by the young person (Foster and Smedley, 2019b).

The result is that the factors that enhance or impede recovery are often two sides of the same coin. Without their own access to the receptive thoughtful mind of an other to help them work through their experiences, the emotional toll of the work can actively corrode care providers' alpha function and undermine their capacity to keep going with emotionally containing approaches. The quality of environment in which the carer is providing care – the availability of support, safety and predictability – contributes significantly to whether the process goes well and to the level of emotional labour that a worker has to invest to mitigate the environment.

Within the reflective practice meeting described in the case example, the first vital task for the facilitator was to accept, validate and show compassionate curiosity about the staff member's expressed feelings, without conveying a sense of judgment that could induce shame. This process, beyond the urgent need to soothe and detoxify the worker's distress, also provides experiential learning for staff of the process of reverie and the container–contained relationship, as well as increasing their bandwidth for what Bion called 'thinking under fire' (Foster, 2020). Having one's worst fears named and accepted along with a provision of a framework in which their varied feelings and responses could be seen as important information about the young person's state of mind opened the door to beginning to think about the situation in more detail.

Whilst the group were still split in their views about whether Colby's episodes were panic attacks, they were able to agree that whatever was happening appeared to overwhelm her in those moments and get in the way of being able to speak out how she was feeling or ask for help. When invited to reflect on moments in Colby's care where staff approaches appeared to work well, staff described episodes in which noticing changes in Colby's affect early on and approaching her with an invite to spend some time together (watching TV, walking in the garden) could sometimes work if they were quick enough. Staff who had been involved in different attempts to try and stop her from creating friction burns on her face thought that talking to her about what they could see and how they imagined she must be feeling seemed to lead to her calming down a little quicker. What was confounding the group was why increasing observation levels seemed to be having the opposite effect.

Bion described reverie as the psychological source of supply for the child's need for love, which as the method for soothing psychological distress is expressed in part by a state of 'receptive observation' (p. 95). The seemingly practical task of observing or knowing a young person's whereabouts within a care environment can provide an important aspect of an emotionally containing environment and reverie through visual transaction (Schore and Schore, 2014). How we are gazed upon and handled by our carers confers love and acceptance.

Alluding to Bion's theory of containment and his own concept of maternal holding, Winnicott described the therapeutic task involved in working with individuals in mental distress as a 'complex derivative of the original face (i.e. the primary carer) whose role it was to reflect back all that the infant/patient brings' (Winnicott, 1971). Fundamental to this is the idea that being seen is the experience of not just being looked at but being taken in, recognized and reflected back by a receptive other, which serves a containing function (Alvarez, 1999). Through this visual interplay comes the installation of an observer within our own minds (sometimes experienced as an internal commentary or voice on our thoughts and actions). In good enough circumstances, this can be thought of as an other who sees us for who we are and still cares for us, whereas in circumstances in which children have not experienced a caregiver's integrative mirroring of their feeling states or their life experiences have disrupted this usual process, they have difficulties creating representations of their own feelings which can lead to difficulties differentiating reality from fantasy and physical from 'psychic' reality (Fonagy, 2003).

Without this, children are left in overwhelming states of anxiety which lead them to rely on primitive or 'infantile' defences (splitting, denial, dissociation, discharging unbearable feelings through aggression to self and other). Even without the additionality of early neglect or deprivation, the presence of acceptant and reflective others in adolescence is especially important because adolescence is characterised by a developmentally normal preoccupation with self-examination in mirror-like or reflective surfaces (both literally and symbolically) in the pursuit of understanding one's emerging identity (Winnicott, 1971). The experience of being looked upon receptively is an invitation to engage (Alvarez, 1999) that also has a bodily experienced component to it that can install a more compassionate appraisal of one's own body-self. Frequent intermittent observations have been shown to provide opportunities for young people to feel seen, taken in and understood (Foster and Smedley, 2019a).

In thinking about the experience of 1:1 observations, group members were able to recognise that although the activity was intended to increase safety and availability of staff by increasing the numbers of staff on a shift, it actually reduced the psychological availability of staff for the other residents, as regular checks usually used to check in with how young people were feeling and to attend to their needs, were being performed in a far more perfunctory manner, as time was limited. Being allocated to 1:1 continuous observation of Colby, also meant staff were not able to respond intuitively to other young people when they passed them and noticed that they were struggling or distressed. This created moral distress in the staff, expressed as anger and resentment towards Colby, and the potential experience of a 'wilfully misunderstanding other' (Bion, 1962a) for the other young people.

Understanding that other residents' increasing challenging behaviours might reflect increased anxiety created opportunity to extend that understanding to the challenging and difficult behaviours the staff were trying to help Colby manage. In a moment of candour, one group member articulated how frustrated and frightened they felt when allocated to Colby's observations and how they managed by effectively checking out and just following the young person around until their time was up. In this situation, the experience of enhanced observations by young people can move from being seen (i.e. needs are recognised, taken in and responded to) to being experienced as being 'looked at' (i.e. surveillance). Opportunities for patient introjection of reverie-based interventions risk getting foreclosed, as the task of doing the observations can become more akin to an 'iron gaze' (Holmes, 2001). Continuous 1:1 observations might provide practical mitigation of risks (though not in this case), but they can also actually reduce the sense of relational security afforded to young people (Foster and Smedley, 2019b).

Given that 1:1 observations were not preventing incidents or helping Colby feel more safe or less distressed, the group agreed to build a list of potential early warning signs of increased distress based on their collective experiences of being with her. They used this to test a plan of using the extra staff to employ intermittent (five-minute) observations, to let her know they always had her in their sights/ thoughts and to actively approach her at the first sign of early warning indicators. The intent was to offer her verbal reflections on how she was presenting and how she might be feeling and to invite her to spend time together. In a parallel process, the reflective practice facilitator temporarily increased the frequency of the group to support the staff with the uncertainty and worry associated with trialling this new plan.

Implications and recommendations

The primary task of enabling developmental growth and reparation for young people who are experiencing complex mental health needs against a backdrop of chronic adversity and complex trauma is fundamentally relational in nature. It requires explicit engagement with young people's felt distress and disturbance, bringing to bear one's own capacity to think about the meaning of these feelings. The case example demonstrates the value that a close application of the details of Bion's theory of thinking can add to understanding the tasks and challenges facing workers in residential care settings for care-experienced young people. Whilst 'The Psycho-Analytic Study of Thinking' is based on technical psychoanalytic theory, the case example demonstrates the potential utility of the psychoanalytic concepts of the container–contained relationship, reverie and projective identification for a non-psychoanalytically trained staff group. These ideas can help staff more clearly understand the needs of the people they care for and move away from concrete appraisals of behaviour, drawing instead on understanding of underlying drivers to modulate their responses.

Work with psychologically distressed adolescents necessarily involves being subject to unconscious communications as young people split off and project feelings for which they have no words or cannot bear (Foster and Smedley, 2019a). Emotional containment has been described as a stepping stone for development of the ability to recognise, tolerate, understand and manage one's own emotional experience (Bion, 1962b). In the context of the care setting described in the example, it means that workers need to be actively receptive to feelings being projected, validate them and de-code their meaning, so that this understanding is available to them and to the adolescent to inform actions or make changes. However, the impact of being continuously up close to such raw distress, disturbance, aggression and trauma can be intensely disturbing and close down staff member's own capacity to sit with and think about their feelings.

Failure to take notice and consider the constitutive elements of the container–contained relationship (reverie, holding, projection, identification and introjection) and the problems that can occur within it, has serious implications for the workforce and for care quality. Care staff will find themselves more vulnerable to burnout and compassion fatigue (Foster, 2018). They are more likely to become unresponsive, or problematically responsive, to unconsciously communicated needs of young people (Foster and Smedley, 2019b). In turn, this can lead to an escalating cycle in which young people excessively rely on projective identification (Bion, 1962b), and staff become concretely identified with mentally distressed adolescent states of mind (Foster, 2009; Foster and Smedley, 2019b).

Drawing parallels between his own experience of combat in World War One and the emotional adversity and intensity that can be associated with working with people with complex mental health needs, Bion wrote, 'In war the enemy's object is to terrify you that you cannot think clearly, while your object is to continue to think clearly no matter how adverse or frightening the situation' (1979, p. 322). Maintenance of the capacity to think under fire requires staff support approaches that are based on exactly the same principles of care for the young people they are looking after. That is, providing emotionally containing spaces and relationships in which staff have access to the receptive observation and thoughtfulness of another mind in order to manage the overwhelming feelings associated with their work and find psychological meaning in the behavioural and psychological disturbances to which they are subjected.

Conclusion

In this chapter, I set out the central tenets of Bion's conceptualisation of how the ability to recognise and tolerate disturbing bodily experiences as emotions with names, thoughts and sensations associated with them emerges from our experiences of being seen, taken in and made sense of by our carers.

This theory of thinking as a fundamental emotional process provides a model for ordinary development, understanding of when this goes awry and the strategies that can be implemented to promote recovery and reparation. It has been applied to understanding behavioural disturbance and psychological distress in children with significant care disruptions. Supporting care staff with the process of naming their work and everyday contribution to care, alongside opportunities for learning about underpinning theory and evidence to help make sense of their and the young people's experiences, and access to supported reflective space in which to think together about their work, can make a significant contribution to helping the residential care staff sustain themselves in the face of the significant demands placed upon them by their work.

References

Alvarez, A. (1999). *Live company*. London: Routledge.
Bion, W. (1959). Attacks on linking. *International Journal Psychoanalysis*, 40, 308–315.

Bion, W. (1962a). The psycho-analytic study of thinking. *International Journal of Psychoanalysis*, 43, 306–311.

Bion, W. (1962b). *Learning from experience*. London: Heinmann.

Bion, W. (1979 [1994]). Making the best of a bad job. In: *Clinical seminars and other works*, 321–331. London: Karnac.

Bion, W.R. (1957). Differentiation of the psychotic from the non-psychotic personalities. *The International Journal of Psychoanalysis*, 38, 266–275.

Bion, W.R. (1958). Development of schizophrenic thought. *The International Journal of Psychoanalysis*, 37, 344–346.

Bower, M. (2005). *Psychoanalytic theory for social work practice: Thinking under fire*. London: Routledge.

Briggs, S. (2009). Risks and opportunities in adolescence: Understanding adolescent mental health difficulties. *Journal of Social Work Practice*, 23(1), 49–64.

Brown, L.J. (2012). Bion's discovery of alpha function: Thinking under fire on the battlefield and in the consulting room. *The International Journal of Psychoanalysis*, 93, 1191–1214. https://doi.org/10.1111/j.1745-8315.2012.00644.x

Cook, A., Spinazzola, J., Ford, J., Lanktree, C., Blaustein, M., Cloitre, M., & Van der Kolk, B. (2005). Complex trauma. *Psychiatric Annals*, 35(5), 390–398.

Fonagy, P. (2003). Mentalization. In: Pfafflin, F., & Adshead, G. (Eds.). *A matter of security: The application of attachment theory to forensic psychiatry and psychotherapy*. London: Jessica Kingsley Publishers.

Foster, C. (2009). Adolescents in acute mental distress on in-patient pediatric settings: Some reflections from a paediatric liaison practitioner. *Journal of Child & Adolescent Psychiatric Nursing*, 22(1), 16–22.

Foster, C. (2018). Investigating professional quality of life in nursing staff working in adolescent psychiatric intensive care units (PICUs). *The Journal of Mental Health Training, Education and Practice*, 14(1), 59–71. https://doi.org/10.1108/JMHTEP-04-2018-0023.

Foster, C. (2020). Evaluating the impact of a psychodynamic work discussion group for mental health nurses in Adolescent PICU. *Archives of Psychiatric Nursing*, 34(6), 481–491. https://doi.org/10.1016/j.apnu.2020.08.008

Foster, C., & Smedley, K. (2019a). Understanding the nature of mental health nursing within CAMH PICU. Part 1: Identifying nursing interventions that contribute to the recovery journey of Young People. *Journal of Psychiatric Intensive Care*, 15(2), 87–102. https://doi.org/10.20299/jpi.2019.012

Foster, C., & Smedley, K. (2019b). Understanding the nature of mental health nursing within CAMH PICU. Part 2: Staff experience and support needs. *Journal of Psychiatric Intensive Care*, 15(2), 103–115. https://doi.org/10.20299/jpi.2019.013

Holmes, D. (2001). From iron gaze to nursing care: Mental health nursing in the era of panopticism. *Journal of Psychiatric and Mental Health Nursing*, 8(1), 7–15. https://10.1046/j.1365-2850.2001.00345.x. PMID: 11879489

Klein, M. (1959 [1975]). Our adult world and its roots in infancy. In: Klein, M. (Ed.). *Envy and gratitude and other works 1946–1963*. Edited by: Masud M., & Khan, R. London: The Hogarth Press.

Ogden, T.H. (2008). Bion's four principles of mental functioning. *Fort Da*, 14(2), 11–35.

Riesenberg-Malcolm, R. (2001). Bion's theory of containment. In: Bronstein, C. (Ed.). *Kleinian theory: A contemporary perspective*. London: Whurr Publishers.

Schore, A., & Schore, J. (2010). Clinical social work and regulation theory: Implications of neurobiological models of attachment. In: Bennett, S., & Nelson, T, (Eds.). *Adult attachment in clinical social work. Essential clinical social work series*. Springer Science.

Schore, J., & Schore, A. (2014). Regulation theory and affect regulation psychotherapy: A clinical primer. *Smith College Studies in Social Work*, 8(2–3), 178–195.

Waddell, M. (2007). Groups of Ganging: The psychodynamics of bullying. *British Journal of Psychotherapy*, 23(2), 189–204.

Waddell, M. (2018). *On adolescence: Inside stories*. Routledge.

Weightman, E., & Smithson, J. (2020). Containment? An investigation into psychoanalytic containment in the NHS in relation to someone with a diagnosis of personality disorder. *Psychoanalytic Psychotherapy*, 33(4), 248–265. https://doi.org/10.1080/02668734.2019.1709537

Winnicott, D. (1971). Mirror-role of mother and family in child development. In: *Playing and reality*. London: Tavistock Publications.

Winship, G., Scott, A. & Edgar, J. (2024). Towards a psychotherapy publishing ethics concordat. *European Journal of Psychotherapy & Counselling*, 26(3–4), 411–427. https://doi.org/10.1080/13642537.2024.2384864

Yakeley, J. (2018). Psychoanalysis in modern mental health practice. *The Lancet Psychiatry*, 5(5), 443–450. https://doi.org/10.1016/S2215-0366(18)30052-X

Going beyond 'Notes on Infant Observation in Psychoanalytic Training' (Bick, 1964)

Promoting sensitivity and attunement in health and social care

Shelly Allen

Introduction

Infant observation has been part of clinical training in psychoanalytic approaches since it was introduced by Esther Bick at The Tavistock Clinic in 1948. It proved foundational and impactful in my own psychodynamic training, where I observed a family with a newborn baby as early after birth as possible. This continued weekly for the first year of the baby's life. The task was to be an unobtrusive observer, open to as much as possible and to capture the experience as closely as able after the weekly observation. Writing up process notes to share in my seminar with other trainees facilitated by a child psychoanalyst allowed meaning to be made, and the experiences evoked were digested. This enabled me to explore my presence during the observation, the relationship between the mother and baby, occasionally with the father and once with an extended family member. The experience enhanced my ability to monitor and contain the feelings it evoked in me. Infant observation was pivotal as I worked towards completing my clinical training, and it has stayed with me ever since.

Whilst infant observation is of a particular kind and is by no means a standard experience offered for those training in health and social care professions, the role that observation has in this context is undeniable. Subtle changes in a person's presentation, childhood developmental milestones, recovery from conditions that impact health and wellbeing, the monitoring and management of risk, a range of physiological measurements – all require observational skills. In this chapter, I will show how the key elements taken from Bick (1964) have transferability to contemporary health and social care practice. To do this, I start with a case example which happened long before I consciously started my clinical training as a psychodynamic psychotherapist.

Case example

Whilst thinking about the proposal for this book, I woke up one morning with a memory that had featured in a dream lodged firmly in my mind. It was not something that I had forgotten – I have used it in teaching with students – but I was

DOI: 10.4324/9781003541660-10

struck by it and not least because this quote kept coming to mind: 'the interpretation of dreams is the royal road to a knowledge of the unconscious activities of the mind' (Freud, 1900, p. 608). The more I thought about my memory and dream, the more an idea came to mind regarding the need for sensitive attunement to deliver high-quality health and social care, not least because on this occasion, being attuned turned out to be lifesaving.

My recollection of it was from a forensic medium-secure unit providing care to people who had mental health problems and had an offending history. It was on a quiet morning, probably a Sunday, when the usual coming and going of the wider clinical team gave way to a less routinised atmosphere. It was during this time that a senior colleague had a sudden sense that something was not right.

The clinical setting was a locked environment; there were two corridors off the main living area at a right angle to each other. The setting was mixed gender, women down one corridor and men the other. There was a predominance of women with a diagnosis of what was termed borderline personality disorder at that time, although not all; there were two women who were experiencing psychosis. The relative proportion of people diagnosed with psychosis to personality disorder in the men's corridor was reversed, with most experiencing psychosis although not exclusively.

It made for a diverse environment with multifaceted needs; there were wide-ranging patient experiences of intrusive and adverse early lives. There were mixed index offences – the offence that brought the person into contact with the criminal justice and then mental health system – including assaults, homicide, arson. There were differences in ethnicity, socio-economic status, education and employment histories. There was a shared legal status; all patients on the unit were subject to Mental Health Act legislation and had no choice but to be there.

My colleague, having had a sense that something was not right, acted on this knowing that "*something*" needed to be checked. She discovered that four of the women had tied ligatures around their necks and were each in the wardrobe of their individual bedrooms. This later became understood as a co-ordinated act of self-harm. I was not there at the time, but I remember hearing about it. My response was relief that the patients had been discovered and that care and intervention could be delivered in a timely way. I was also relieved that I had not been there, mixed with a sense of respect for my colleague who had felt the need and checked. It raised questions for me such as how she had known to do this, what was being communicated and what it all meant.

With distance to reflect, and guided by my psychotherapy training, I now had ideas about these questions from my perspective, but I was interested in thinking more. I decided to go back to my colleague to see if she could recall the event, what had happened and how she felt at the time.

The first thing to say is that this happened many years ago, and yet we can both remember it; the significance of this memory not being lost on either of us. So much of what I just described was shared; the part that was new in our discussion was the impact of the event. My colleague recalls a sense of disquiet which prompted her to ask other staff if they had seen the four women recently, when no one confirmed they had, disquiet turned to an increasing concern that something was wrong. My colleague and others went to check the bedrooms, it was here that the four women were found. The alarm was raised for a medical emergency. the sound of the alarm and of members of staff responsible for responding to these events, being a significant memory that was recalled in our discussion.

During our discussion, it was apparent that the impact remained present even after so many years. My colleague described the distress experienced, the rising sense of panic on finding the first woman and thinking, Are the others in their wardrobes? whilst concurrently believing they would not be. When reflecting on the incident, this sense of disbelief continued that they would coordinate such an act. Sibling rivalry was a thought that came to my colleague's mind, reinforcing the bewilderment that the four women had come together in this way, knowing intervention would then be shared across the group rather than focused individually. Feelings of responsibility were described and relief that all four women survived the incident, alongside the concern that the situation could have been fatal. My colleague thought they must have known they would be saved, or that they could all have died; she wondered how that might have been understood, and further considered if one of the women had died: who would be to blame? who was the ring leader? She concluded 'guess we'll never know'. It prompted my colleague to consider if it had been planned or a concerted attack on staff and ask the question, 'Did they hate us?'

The earliest example of non-verbal communication is between a baby and their caregiver; infant observation is a crucial part of psychodynamic training. The nuanced, sometimes subtle, at other times explosive, communication is part of the trainee's development in being able to appreciate and tolerate nonverbal, primitive, unconscious communication. This is not reserved for psychodynamic approaches; this is an everyday occurrence in how we communicate. In considering this in the context of health and social care settings, how we respond to this unconscious communication and its impact on us is crucial. Bearing what is being communicated and evoked in the practitioner to allow something to come into view so that it can be thought about is key, as this case example illustrates. Before advancing the themes raised in the case example, I provide an overview of Bick's (1964) 'Notes on Infant Observation'.

Overview of the paper

Esther Bick's 'Notes on Infant Observation in Psychoanalytic Training' (1964) details the use of this experience to encourage close attention, meaning making through observation and monitoring of one's own experiences when in repeated contact with mothers and their babies. Its importance can be seen in the influence of this paper, having been cited thousands of times and referred to in numerous texts. It has been an element of psychoanalytic/dynamic training at the Tavistock Clinic since 1948, and it remains a part of clinical training today.

The nature, purpose, and method of infant observation, with the accompanying seminar, is introduced by Bick (1964). The importance of consecutive observation in building up an understanding of what is being communicated, how and why, is stressed:

> The experience of the seminar is that one may see an apparent pattern emerging in one observation, but one can only accept it as significant if it is repeated in the same, or a similar, situation in many subsequent observations. Paying attention to such observable details over a long period gives the student the opportunity to see not only patterns but also changes in the patterns.
>
> (p. 116)

The use of the experience in finding ways to talk to mothers about their child's history is highlighted as a function of infant observation and how this is then transferable to the wider context of practice. Bick also stresses the opportunity for the observer to witness how relationships develop within families and to deepen this experience through the use of the seminar where participants join in the pursuit of meaning making.

The importance of its inclusion in being able to take a developmental perspective in psychoanalytically informed training is summed up here:

> help the students to conceive vividly the infantile experience of their child patients, so that when, for example, they started the treatment of a two-and-a-half years' old child they would get the feel of the baby that he was and from which he is not so far removed.
>
> (Bick, 1964, p. 106)

'Notes on Infant Observation' includes excerpts from observations and the concepts of 'holding' as Winnicott understood it and Bion's 'containment' are brought to life in relation to the babies that are presented in the paper. The experience of holding and containment in the student can also be inferred in the passage where Bick comments on learning to watch and feel before jumping in, tolerating and appreciating difference to one's own perceptions and views of how something should be. Essentially the individual nature of the mother and infant, how the baby develops at its own pace and relates to itself and its mother in its own unique way. The transferability of the concepts in this paper beyond infant observation is summed up by the following quote:

> I think that the infant observation experience, linked later with clinical experience with adults and children, will add to their conviction of the importance of observing patients' overall behaviour as a part of the data of the analytic situation as well as strengthen their belief in the validity of analytic reconstructions of early development.
>
> (p. 122)

Discussion

Containing and holding

When I introduce containment and holding to health and social care students, I use an analogy by asking students to recall a time on placement when they were asked to do something they had not done before. It usually helps if students can think about a particular task in which they lacked confidence; this tends to be a universal experience. I then ask them to think about their supervisor who asked them to complete the task with no guidance or support, I encourage students to say how this feels.

It tends to stir up anxiety, concern about getting it wrong, illustrating their lack of skill and knowledge related to the task and feeling helpless to invoke the support of their supervisor. I then ask them to think more long term about how this might impact them. Often students will say they experience a reluctance to engage in the placement experiences, a worry that they are not being supported; they may feel angry and impeded in their development. The experience of anxiety may lead to avoidance or, conversely, feeling unable to say no to the task for fear of looking like they do not know what they are doing and how it might reflect on their assessment. This latter strategy has potential consequences not just for the student if they perform a task for which they are ill equipped. This example serves to illustrate how if the student's anxiety is not being contained and the environment in which they find themselves is not one of holding, they are left to fend for themselves without the help of their supervisor.

I then ask students to recall a time when they were supported by their supervisor and ask them to share the experience; contrary to the first example, this evokes feelings of safety, being able to take the next step knowing there is guidance and support should they falter, and a shared experience when it goes right. This tends to provide a foundation from which the student says they can progress, knowing they have somewhere to go when feeling overwhelmed or uncertain. Developmentally, this is crucial for us all.

I link this to formative experiences to show the importance of good enough care – to use Winnicott's term – and, conversely, the lifelong impacts of early experiences that lacked elements of containment and holding. These may result from caregivers' absence, mental health problems, issues with substance use, trauma and abuse. The consequences of these difficult early experiences may manifest in a number of ways including mental health issues and patterns of offending as referred to in the case example.

Providing containment and a holding environment relies on an openness in the caregiver to be receptive to the internal state of the infant. It is only in being moved by this unconscious communication from the baby that care will result, for instance the high, shrill cry of a child that needs to be fed, prompts action in the caregiver under good enough circumstances. It is not an exaggeration to state that survival for all of us has depended upon this. It is also a mechanism which we all rely on throughout life; feeling psychically held and having our anxiety contained by another when it threatens to overwhelm us, again in good enough circumstances, is something we all rely on in times of distress.

The case example can be understood as a communication of distress through action, the use of the body being highly significant here. Freud (1923) stated that the ego is first and foremost a bodily ego. This means, as in the example of the hungry baby, that our awareness of needs, gratification and frustration are first felt bodily before we can developmentally turn them into a thought. My colleague's observation that something was not right moved her to act on this; using her own inner resources and managing her anxiety, she was able to mobilise herself and the staff group into action, which in this case was lifesaving.

Women in forensic mental health care

The women referred to in the case example at the beginning of this chapter were all classed as restricted patients, defined as

> a mentally disordered offender (MDO) subject to a restriction order, due to the risk of serious harm they pose to others, and liable to a hospital order. They cannot be transferred between hospitals, discharged or allowed leave without consent of the Secretary of State for Justice.

> (Ministry of Justice, 2024a)

Whilst I was writing this chapter, the information concerning restricted patients for England & Wales in the UK was updated in April 2024 and drew on figures for 2023. There were 7,833 restricted patients up to 31 December 2023; this comprised 4,648 restricted patients in hospitals and 3,185 who were conditionally discharged. About 88% of all restricted patients were males, and 14% females, who comprised 14% of the conditionally discharged population and 10% of the detained population (Ministry of Justice, 2024b).

As shown in these statistics, women in receipt of forensic care are a minority group. Most evidence-based practice has been derived from research with men, the needs of women within this type of facility subsumed by the majority. The women referred to in the case example all had documented adverse childhood experiences and challenging life events. In recognising the levels of adversity experienced by the four women, the intention is not to collapse them into a homogenous group, but in trying to maintain confidentiality, there is a need for sensitive portrayal of relevant information.

Two of the four women had spent time in high-secure provision, although in keeping with patterns reported in the wider available evidence, for lesser offences than their male counterparts. One had never had contact with secondary mental health services before their index offence resulted in admission to medium-secure forensic services. Demographically, they had all finished school by the age of 16, and most had very little paid employment. One woman identified as having a mixed ethnic background and the other three as white.

None of the four women had sustained relationships with intimate partners, family or friends and did not regularly receive visitors. One had been in a relationship with a man she had met in forensic mental health care who had died by suicide. Their ages ranged from late teens to 40s. The index offences included arson and violence to others, and actual bodily harm was the most severe; all four shared a diagnosis of borderline, now termed emotionally unstable personality disorder. One had had a child removed, placed into care and later adopted. These were women with differences and similarities as might be expected, but one of the things they shared was a history of trauma.

Whilst gender-specific corridors with individual bedrooms linked to a shared communal living area allowed a degree of separation, the men who occupied this space had also committed violent offences towards others which included multiple homicides, rape and child sexual abuse. The intention is not to portray a simple gender-based comparison here; women are capable of violence and cruelty just as men are, and males who end up in criminal justice and forensic mental health services are more likely to have had a history of trauma (Ali & Adshead, 2022), but in terms of the case example and trying to understand the dynamic, these were the circumstances. Available information also reflects the evidence which indicates that

> the needs of violent women resemble those for violent men in terms of common risk factors, especially previous mental health issues, early childhood adversity and substance misuse. However, there may(be) important differences in terms of the level of physical violence inflicted on others and women's apparently increased willingness to direct violence to their own bodies in the form of self-harming behaviour.
>
> (Ali & Adshead, 2022, p. 7)

Reflection on the situation described in the case example is with a sense of regret; as much as we had tried to provide a safe, therapeutic space, we could not account for the experiences evoked for the women living in proximity with men who represented the trauma they had endured and/or witnessed. No matter what we did, this was a pervasive part of the experience. Added to this was the discourse that having a diagnosed mental illness was far greater justification for care and treatment than a diagnosis of personality disorder. Not only had these four women been disempowered and disenfranchised even before coming into contact with forensic mental health services, but in the opinion of some, their perceived right to care and treatment diminished in comparison with those who were psychotic. Looking back, I can now see that aspects of the setting replicated patterns of earlier experiences of trauma, abuse, disempowerment and rejection. When my colleague asked 'did they hate us' I think yes, that was part of it.

Being attuned to all communication

To feel that one is on the receiving end of another's hatred and not retaliate is crucial in health and social care. It is a point made by Winnicott (1949) in urging acceptance that those providing care will also hate their patients. Winnicott encourages consideration of this so it can be thought about and managed rather than intruding and negatively impacting on the relationship and work with the patient.

People who use health and social services bring complexity related to their trauma; these early experiences manifest in relationships in the present. Young and Stubley (2022) comment that one consequence of trauma is that the person may want help but also fear it given past abuse by those who were meant to care. This relates to the complex communication represented in the case example where there was a sense of hatred being communicated. Hate in this context can be considered in terms of a transference relationship. Directing hatred towards the staff could be hypothesised as a re-enactment in the form of a retaliation towards those who were tasked to care in early life but abused this. There is also an added element of jeopardy in relation to the use of ligatures, giving staff a time limited opportunity to intervene. This could be understood as a measure of how much staff care, testing whether the four women were held in mind.

In recounting the incident that forms the case example for this chapter, we understood this as a co-ordinated act of self-harm. It is worth thinking about the chosen method of this given this is a communication in itself. Turp (2003) states that self-harm is an umbrella term for behaviour that leads to physical harm to the self either by commission or omission. It breaches socially and culturally accepted norms and elicits a strong emotional response as a result. This definition derives from Turp's (2003) criticism that self-harm is often too narrowly characterised as a high-visibility act and instead stresses the importance of considering the underlying states of mind which precipitate harm to the self.

There are times when the underlying state of mind is clearly articulated, self-harm described as a way of managing difficulty as opposed to a desire to die. However, Campbell and Hale (2017) make the point that ligature use is less clear and has elements of both these states of mind. The complexity that this evokes for those providing care is clear; if it is about a desire to die and a desire to stay alive, it brings into question how to respond.

Sitting with uncertainty for those who work in health and social care can be extremely anxiety provoking. There are occasions where it is clear that action needs to be taken as detailed in the case example. However, not all situations benefit from this. There are times where watchful waiting in an engaged state is required to allow for understanding what is being communicated to adequately unfold.

Watchful unfolding

Whilst health and social care environments are undoubtedly high pressured with the need to make decisions and take action, as illustrated in the case example, life-threatening situations excluded, being quick to act can have limitations. It is not only the containment of others' anxiety that is so important but also that of the practitioner.

The need to find space to think and consider allows an opportunity for the issue at hand to be engaged with more fully. In so doing, there is less risk of being pushed

or pulled into taking up a particular position, for instance through projective identification and enactments. The ability to sit with the associated feelings this evokes
can be uncomfortable, and at times very difficult to bear, particularly when others are waiting for a decision or expectantly wanting an answer. The ability to
observe in an open-minded way without hasty intervention is a vital part of Bick's
approach. In relation to this, Reid (1997, p. 1) describes it as follows: 'to see what
there is to be seen and not to look for what they think should be there'.

Taking up this approach as 'a modest guest', Abrahamsen, (2018) describes an
unobtrusive, non-interfering person. Whilst this is not applicable in all situations,
it can be helpful to borrow this approach from infant observation in enabling connection with the impact of the work in health and social care and monitoring one's
own responses.

Returning to the case example, it is significant that many years later, feelings
of fear and distress are still activated when thinking about this event. Barnard and
Jones (2022) state that regardless of modality or approach, reflection and containment are key to managing the impact of working with traumatised people, particularly where there is potential for the practitioner to be subject to vicarious trauma.

Undertaking an infant observation as described in 'Notes on Infant Observation'
Bick (1964) cannot extend to all preparation for working in health and social care,
but the importance of what it teaches deserves a place for consideration. It is also
notable that it has been adapted and used in contexts beyond those oriented around
psychoanalytic and psychodynamic training. Hingley-Jones, Parkinson and Allain
(2016) describe a 12-week infant observation based on Bick (1964) to support
undergraduate and postgraduate qualifying programmes in social work.

The impact of this approach was also detailed by Hall (2008), who was a staff
nurse on a children's cancer ward and undertook infant observation. It was concluded that acknowledgement of the traumatic nature of the work and the need for
holding in terms of the staff providing care for children with cancer was imperative. Further, regular support or a discussion group was welcome in safeguarding
the well-being of all involved where the painful reality of the children's experiences could be acknowledged and supported.

Implications and recommendations

Underpinning education with psychodynamic perspectives

The inclusion of infant observations and psychodynamic perspectives in education
programmes across different disciplines is varied. For example, in a counselling
or psychotherapy course, some elements of this would be expected to an extent,
and similarly in medical psychotherapy courses. Social work may be more diverse
in terms of its inclusion; elsewhere in this book, we discuss this in one master's
course leading to social work qualification, but it cannot be stated with confidence
that a psychodynamic stance is adopted wholesale.

This is regrettable given that in their analysis of student feedback, Hingley-Jones,
Parkinson and Allain (2016) identified three ways in which baby and young child

observation contributes to learning which can be seen to apply across all health and social care professions. Students engage with and learn about the complexity of child development; observing facilitates the development of crucial skill acquisition, and students described how they developed the capacity to take up and maintain professionalism.

This finding from a decade ago remains relevant when put into a global context and where observational skills and the ability to bear what is noticed and stirred up is required to support judicious decision-making and acting with integrity. Global statistics suggest that six in 10, or 400 million children under the age of five, regularly suffer physical punishment and/or psychological violence at the hands of parents and caregivers. One in five women and one in seven men report having been sexually abused as a child (UNICEF, 2024).

Independent Inquiry Child Sexual Abuse (2022) draws on evidence stating that the average time for victims and survivors to disclose sexual abuse is 26 years. Barriers to disclosure are wide reaching and include victim blaming and being too young at the time to recognise or not having the language to describe abuse. Community leaders occasionally restrict access to support, not recognising the cultural and religious needs of people from racially minoritised communities. Under-reporting of child sexual abuse in LGBTQ+ communities and prejudices regarding looked-after children who disclose sexual abuse also make it more difficult to get help.

Those who work in health and social care have opportunistic contact across all communities and are in an ideal position to support disclosures of abuse and mobilise help and support. To do this requires an openness to all aspects of communication, including the unconscious, to be attuned when something is not right and to be able to manage the anxiety stirred up when abuse is suspected and disclosed and act as a result. Being able to bear and act accordingly in this context requires help and support through preparation, with education being the ideal opportunity for this.

Supporting learning through experience

Bick's (1964) paper, the case example and the preceding discussion all make the point about learning from experience. Earlier I referred to the nonverbal communication between a baby and their caregiver, as nuanced and sometimes subtle and at other times as explosive. Developmentally, we have all relied on the attention of our caregivers to ensure that our needs are met. This requires the baby's raw communication, screams, cries, motor movements such as scrunching up the body to be translated by the caregiver. In good enough conditions, the need as it has been expressed and understood can be attended to. With repeated experiences and development, the child begins to take on this function for themselves. This is something Bion (1962), considered in his theory of thinking:

> It is convenient to regard thinking as dependent on the successful outcome of two main mental developments. The first is the development of thoughts. They

require an apparatus to cope with them. The second development, therefore, is of this apparatus that I shall provisionally call thinking. I repeat-thinking has to be called into existence to cope with thoughts.

(p. 306)

Bion referred to beta elements as the raw, unprocessed bodily experiences which are then translated into alpha elements through this apparatus of thinking. It requires maternal reverie and containment to support this process and in times of distress we all need someone to support us in this way.

It is in the pursuit of supporting learning through experiences that the critique by Ballatt, Campling and Maloney (2020, p. 37), can be addressed: 'too often, the attention of educators, managers and staff is directed to the technical, the performative elements of the clinical or caring task, rather than the relational'. From an educative perspective, my own practice in attending to this criticism includes supporting the inclusion of psychodynamic thinking in a master's programme leading to qualification in social work at a UK university. Co-facilitating a psychoanalytically informed reading group with psychological practitioners, psychotherapists, undergraduate and postgraduate students and university staff and running psychodynamic work discussion groups, all of which are discussed in more detail in this book. Essentially these are reflective spaces for exploring and digesting the impact of working in health and social care, much like the importance stressed in Bick (1964) regarding the function of the seminar for infant observation.

Space to digest and work through

As acknowledged earlier, infant observation and its exploration through the accompanying seminar is not standard throughout health and social care education and practice. However, there are opportunities to make good use of reflection, Evans (2021) makes the point that feeling overwhelmed by the nature of the work and its impact is less likely to happen if supportive management structures are in place, which include supervision, clinical discussion, reflective practice and effective leadership.

This was explored by Yiu et al. (2025) specifically in relation to mental health in-patient settings. Interestingly, this qualitative research included perspectives gained from both facilitators and participants experiences. It was found that reflective practice groups may assist in the communication of difficult emotions at work and enhance emotional competence. Team morale was boosted and a sense of connectedness was established with an improvement in team dynamics.

An established approach to psychodynamic practice and training, the work discussion group also warrants consideration here. Youell (2024) explores this with participants on a course which was not explicitly psychoanalytic in its orientation. This fits well with the premise here that learning from experience underpins the work discussion method. Youell describes the work discussion seminar as being honest, open and far reaching, although not necessarily reassuring. This can be seen to protect against what Cardona, (2020, p. 68) refers to as a culture of positiveness which shields against negative projections, despite participation in work discussion being unsettling at times, it is this authentic experience which makes it so worthwhile,

> 'the most important thing about a work discussion group for her is that it makes you stop for a moment . . . to stop and to think'
>
> (Youell, 2024, p. 137).

Conclusion

In this chapter, I have shown how the role of observation in health and social care is a central tenet on which high-quality practice rests. Using 'Notes on Infant Observation in Psychoanalytic Training' (Bick, 1964) and the case example to organise the discussion, implications and recommendations, I considered much of what preoccupies practitioners in health and social care. This links to the impact of the work, the holding and containment of anxiety and concerns about risk, the need for thoughtful, well considered educative experiences to support practitioners in their preparation and maintenance of high-quality practice has been considered.

I acknowledge that infant observation is not a standard experience open to all who work in health and social care; however, I stress that there are fundamental benefits in appreciating it as an approach which links to education, learning from experience and securing reflective spaces to digest and process the emotional impact of the work to support the delivery of high quality health and social care.

References

Abrahamsen, G.R. (2018). Up against the wall. *Infant Observation*, 21(1), 33–47.
Ali, S., & Adshead, G. (2022). Just like a woman: Gender role stereotypes in forensic psychiatry. *Frontiers in Psychiatry*, 13.
Ballatt, J., Campling, P., & Maloney, C. (2020). *Intelligent Kindness: Rehabilitating the Welfare State*. 2nd ed. Cambridge University Press.
Barnard, L., & Jones, J. (2022). Bridging the gap: Developing a thinking space for refugees. In Stubley, J., & Young, L. (Eds.), *Complex Trauma the Tavistock Model*. London & New York. Routledge Taylor Francis Group.
Bick, E. (1964). Notes on infant observation. In Harris, M., & Bick, E. (Ed.), *The Tavistock Model Collected Papers of Martha Harris & Esther Bick*. London. The Harold Meltzer Trust.
Bion, W.R. (1962, Jan 1). A theory of thinking. *The International Journal of Psycho-Analysis*, 43.
Campbell, D., & Hale, R. (2017). *Working in the Dark Understanding the Pre-Suicide State of Mind*. London & New York. Routledge Taylor Francis Group.
Cardona, F. (2020). *Work Matters Consulting to Leader Sand Organizations in the Tavistock Tradition*. London & New York. Routledge Taylor & Francis Group.
Evans, M. (2021). *Psychoanalytic Thinking in Mental Health Settings*. London & New York. Routledge Taylor & Francis Group.

Freud, S. (1900). *The Interpretation of Dreams in the Standard Edition of the Complete Psychological Works of Sigmund Freud*, vols. 4–5, translated and edited by Strachey, J. London. Hogarth Press.

Freud, S. (1923). *The Ego and the Id*. Standard Edition. 19.

Hall, A. (2008). Trauma and containment in children's cancer treatment. *International Journal of Infant Observation*, 6(2), 111–127.

Hingley-Jones, H., Parkinson, C., & Allain, L. (2016). 'Back to our roots?' Re-visiting psychoanalytically-informed baby and young child observation in the education of student social workers. *Journal of Social Work Practice*, 30(3), 249–265. https://doi.org/10.1080/02650533.2016.1215974

IndependentInquiry Child Sexual Abuse. (2022). https://www.iicsa.org.uk/document/report-independent-inquiry-child-sexual-abuse-october-2022-0.html Accessed 30th April 2025.

Ministry of Justice (2024a). https://assets.publishing.service.gov.uk/media/6628dd5bdb4b9f0448a7e583/Notes_and_Definitions_-_Restricted_Patients_Statistics.pdf#:~:text=A%20restricted%20patient%20is%20a%20mentally%20disordered,of%20the%20Secretary%20of%20State%20for%20Justice. Accessed 30th April 2025.

Ministry of Justice (2024b). https://assets.publishing.service.gov.uk/media/6628f32bb0ace32985a7e63a/Restricted_Patients_Statistics_2023.pdf Accessed 30th April 2025.

Reid, S. (Ed.). (1997). *Developments in Infant Observation: The Tavistock Model*. London: Routledge.

Turp, M. (2003). *Hidden Self-Harm Narratives from Psychotherapy*. London and Philadelphia. Jessica Kingsley Publishers.

UNICEF. (2024). https://www.unicef.org/press-releases/nearly-400-million-young-children-worldwide-regularly-experience-violent-discipline accessed 30th April 2025.

Winnicott, D.W. (1949). Hate in the counter-transference. *The International Journal of Psycho-Analysis*, 30, 69–74.

Yiu, P.L.J., McDonogh, A., Gill, H., & Billings, J. (2025). Creating a culture, not just a space – a qualitative investigation into reflective practice groups in inpatient mental health settings from the perspectives of facilitators and attendees. *PLoS ONE*, 20(1), e0316030. https://doi.org/10.1371/journal.pone.0316030

Youell, B. (2024). Introducing psychoanalytic observation through work discussion: The relationship between experiential learning and theory. *Infant Observation*, 27(2), 130–138. https://doi.org/10.1080/13698036.2024.2443883

Young, L., & Stubley, J. (2022). Introduction. In Stubley, J., & Young, L. (Eds.)- Op cit.

Chapter 10

On meeting our 'Ghosts in the Nursery' (Fraiberg, Adelson, & Shapiro, 1975)

Shelly Allen and Pat Cartney

Introduction

In this chapter, we take concepts from Fraiberg, Adelson, and Shapiro's (1975) 'Ghosts in the Nursery: A Psychoanalytic Approach to the Problems of Impaired Infant–Mother Relationships' to present the idea that 'ghosts' from the past found in the nursery exert their influence generationally in the here and now, impacting our current relationships and how we understand our contemporary selves. This understanding is particularly important in health and social care practice and education. We propose that psychodynamic approaches informed by 'Ghosts in the Nursery' offer a framework for in-depth understanding and support humane, thoughtful care (Evans, 2021). An appreciation that past ghosts have contributed to difficult early experiences can assist in formulating an understanding of distress and mental health issues, which Evans (2021) links with problems settling into education, employment and enjoying long-term, satisfying relationships.

Such problems are not confined to those who seek assistance from health and social care; it is important to acknowledge that this is not a one-way relationship. These ghosts are present in all that the practitioner brings with them too. A lack of awareness that this is a key dynamic between the person accessing the service and the practitioner can hinder progress and even be damaging. Therefore, it is crucial to reflect on what one brings to such relationships to understand where there may be an identification with the person accessing services which could result in an unconscious draw to respond in ways that lack thought and purposeful action.

It is with the intention of supporting students who are working towards becoming social workers that these approaches have been incorporated into their programme of study, which we will detail to offer context. It is also incumbent upon us to acknowledge that as educators we also bring our ghosts to our work with students. In this chapter, we will articulate how reflection on the concepts from 'Ghosts in the Nursery' can build on a psychodynamic foundation for practice. This helps underpin thoughtful and humane responses to those accessing services and supports high-quality education within contemporary health and social care.

DOI: 10.4324/9781003541660-11

Case example

Social work has a long history at the University of Manchester, with the first certificate of social work course offered in 1912. The current social work MA attracts applicants from a diverse population, nationally and internationally and maintains a strong focus on helping students to link theory and practice and demonstrate their skills in practice settings. There has always been a theory and practice unit as a key component of teaching on the programme and for many years psychodynamic thinking has been taught as one way of helping students to make sense of some of the complex situations and emotions experienced in the practice arena.

In recent years, the increased complexity of practice (Shdaimah & Strier, 2020), alongside the challenges faced because of neo-liberal welfare agendas (Fenton, 2020) and austerity policies (British Association of Social Work, 2023), has placed particular challenges on social work practice and assessment (Eaton, 2025). A key challenge for contemporary social work educators is how best to support students to integrate relevant theoretical knowledge and skills in the increasingly demanding and unpredictable practice context which is typical of all health and social care provision.

We believe that psychodynamic thinking can offer social work students an effective way of processing some of the multi-layered complexity in practice that students both experience and are required to attend to. Our thinking about how to effectively incorporate these ideas into the classroom began with this underlying premise and drew on the work of Ferguson (2018) and Osborne, Salzberger-Wittenberg, and Williams (1993) as underpinning knowledge.

Ferguson's (2018) ethnographic study of social work practice on child protection visits explored the concept of reflective practice as a core tenet of teaching in health and social care. He drew upon psychoanalytic thinking to argue that whilst social workers were able to 'reflect in action' (Schon, 1992) in some circumstances, there were other situations where 'non- reflection arose to protect the worker . . . in what I will call the defended nature of the self' (Ferguson, 2018, p. 416). The key argument here is that in order 'to make work bearable and doable' (p. 424), there are situations where social workers defend themselves against the emotional impact of the work and their resulting high anxiety. Whilst this was noted as being pragmatically useful in the short run, in some situations, the dangers of this as a long-term strategy were highlighted as leading to potentially defensive and poor practice.

Ferguson saw high-quality supervision where supervisors offer containment and promote critical thinking as a key way of moving forward in this context. He also tasked social work educators with the need to help students to develop their ability to contain their own emotions to tolerate the increased anxiety that may arise in difficult situations, and to allow space for vital insights into the service user experience and the helping process to emerge. The authors of this chapter focused on Fraiberg, Adelson, & Shapiro (1975) and worked together to plan teaching sessions with the explicit aim of seeking to address this educational task.

We draw upon the thinking of Osborne, Salzberger-Wittenberg, and Williams (1993) to sensitise us to the complex emotional context in which learning and teaching happens. The authors use psychoanalytic concepts from Bion and Klein in relation to projective identification and containment, with Winnicott's ideas about holding to illuminate aspects of teacher–student relationships and interactions. We have remained sensitive to the operation of such processes and how feelings from student cohorts, particularly anxiety, uncertainty and being overwhelmed, can be projected onto lecturers seeking to encourage students to tolerate anxiety and uncertainty.

Such projections and other defence mechanisms can also be exhibited in peer-to-peer interactions as a way of seeking to manage anxiety and not knowing in relation to learning processes. As lecturers facilitating the group learning, we are aware of the need to explore and process countertransference responses which can emerge as part of the group interactions. Osborne, Salzberger-Wittenberg, and Williams (1993) highlight how educators have conscious aspirations and fears that we bring to our teaching environments but adds,

> we are also likely to carry into the situation attitudes unbeknown to us. The latter form part of the internal picture of relationships and will powerfully influence our perception and behaviour. We never completely outgrow infantile wishes and attitudes and they are bound to some extent to invade our private and intimate relationships. It is important, however, that we strive to become aware of them so as to minimise their interference in our professional life.
>
> (p. 41)

The classroom in this context is a hotbed of interrelating ghosts from all our pasts which impacts learning about the ghosts of others in practice contexts. The current MA teaching iteration consists of two asynchronous lectures designed to offer students a grounding in core principles on the application of psychodynamic thinking and using defence mechanisms. A workshop is then organised around working with the themes of the unconscious, object relations, defence mechanisms and difference. After students have started their practice placements, they also engage in two skills-focused longer workshop sessions. These sessions explicitly focus on using psychodynamic approaches to support formulation in practice contexts; in the second workshop, students are encouraged to bring their own practice experiences for peer discussion.

Formulation is used as a framework to support the co-creation of a hypothesis about what is happening in practice situations to inform interventions. Students are encouraged to present hypotheses about the way a person's conscious and unconscious thoughts and feelings may have developed and may cause or contribute to their difficulties (Psychodynamic Formulation Collective, 2022). Students are invited to use psychodynamic formulations as tools to develop working hypotheses of difficulties by condensing information into a coherent, meaningful and sensitive account of the core issues that service users are experiencing. Students are

encouraged to explore issues fully, to hold on to uncertainty and not to seek definitive explanations but rather to acknowledge complexity and fluidity. This is supported with an underpinning that appreciates that psychodynamic formulations do
not offer definitive explanations but can shift and change over time as new thinking
and knowledge emerges.

A key component of learning at this stage is supporting students to identify their
responses and reactions to the service user's material. Placing this in the context
of countertransference reactions and pulls towards certain actions to prevent concretely playing these dynamics out in their practice (Polnay et al., 2023).

We seek to provide an overview of key psychodynamic concepts and ways of
working with these ideas to help us understand overarching social work processes
and practices. It is in this context that ideas from 'Ghosts in the Nursery' can make
sense to social work students, as we encourage consideration of how ghosts from the
past can influence current day interactions between social workers and service users.

Overview of the paper

'Ghosts in the Nursery' opens with the statement 'In every nursery there are ghosts',
which introduces the idea that past experiences of being parented impact the current
relationship with one's own children. This idea is then extended to take account of
families where bonds are said to be strong and stable and where the influence of the
past may intrude briefly. This intrusion may prompt seeking advice in areas such
as feeding, sleep, toilet training and discipline, these being linked with particular
parental vulnerabilities and are often transient issues. Attention is then turned in
the paper to those families 'who appear to be possessed by their ghosts' (Fraiberg,
Adelson & Shapiro, 1975, p. 388) and the work of the Infant Mental Health Program on which the paper is based.

It is stated that by the time families come to access the service, the baby is
already in peril, emotionally starved and developmentally impaired:

> In each of these cases, the baby has become a silent partner in a family tragedy.
> The baby in these families is burdened by the oppressive past of his parents from
> the moment he enters the world. The parent, it seems, is condemned to repeat the
> tragedy of his childhood with his own baby in terrible and exacting detail.
> (Fraiberg, Adelson & Shapiro, 1975, p. 388)

Fraiberg, Adelson and Shapiro (1975) observe that these parents may not
approach the service for assistance, referring to those families who have lived
with their ghosts for three or more generations, and who are more likely to regard
the professionals as the intruders, not the ghosts. The paradox is noted whereby
a family history of tragedy, cruelty and sorrow exists and yet does not interfere
with providing the child the care they need. The relationship between those who
have suffered yet find healing in their experience of being a parent and those who
inflict their earlier pain on their children is complex. It is stated in the paper that

history is not destiny and the reader is urged to consider the multitude of factors that determine repetition in the present.

'Ghosts in the Nursery' is underpinned by Freud's (1914) contention regarding the repetition of the past in the present. It is not the first two groups of families described by Fraiberg, Adelson and Shapiro that cause most concern, parents who are subject to brief intruders or unwelcome ghosts which temporarily exert their influence. It is the families who are invaded by their ghosts that then take up residence that are cause for concern.

The paper focuses on the authors' work as part of what came to be called the Infant Mental Health Program, drawing on perspectives from psychoanalytic thinking, developmental psychology and social work. These approaches are used to understand the events of the past with undoing their damaging impacts the main goal of the work. This is illustrated through the cases of two babies and their families.

Attachment is made explicit in the discussion around parents and babies, but the other theme to be mindful of in this chapter is the response of parents and the wider family to the available help. The strong alliance forged between parents/family and workers to banish the impact of past ghosts is contrasted with the parental experience that the intruders are not the ghosts in the nursery but the perceived meddlesome workers. This is advanced and resolved in the paper by detailing the level of engagement achieved by workers. Their ability to hold issues of risk in a thoughtful way without resorting to defensive practice and sticking with families who have multifaceted complexities which had the potential to repeat past experiences in the most damaging ways. The links to work within contemporary health and social care are undeniable in this respect. It is often the impact of these multifaceted complexities alongside the influence of hidden ghosts that social work students need support to hold and critically understand in order to humanely move forward with those they are supporting.

The impact of 'Ghosts in the Nursery' is illustrated not just by its thousands of citations but by its legacy, drawing on psychoanalytic theory, in offering an understanding of how the parental past has the potential to hijack the baby's experiences of being loved and cared for. In the paper, this is brought to life through the experiences of two babies, Mary and Greg. Mary had come to the Infant Mental Health Program at 5 ½ months after her mother had asked for Mary to be adopted, only to have this prevented by her husband who refused consent. The second baby highlighted in the paper is Greg, who the team were called to urgently assess at 3 ½ months. Greg was living with his 16-year-old mother, Annie, who was neglecting to care for him and his 19-year-old father, Earl. Annie was said to be the third generation of mothers in her family who had abandoned their babies, and it was Annie's mother, Greg's grandmother, who called for help, movingly saying 'I don't want to see what happened to me and my babies happen to Annie and her baby' (Fraiberg, Adelson & Shapiro, 1975, p. 403). The main tenets of this paper can be seen as underpinning contemporary approaches to supporting parents and infants with examples such as perinatal mental health services, mother and baby units, safeguarding procedures and family support services.

Discussion

Having summarised the main aspects of the paper to inform this chapter, attention now turns to the meeting of our ghosts and the implications this may have between service user and practitioner, and educator and student drawing on the case example previously detailed.

As discussed, one of the main points in 'Ghosts in the Nursery' (Fraiberg, Adelson, and Shapiro, 1975) is that these ghosts impact on the parenting of one's own children. In this chapter, we are drawing on this whilst also extending the focus beyond this formative relationship to take account of the much broader context of health and social care practice. We argue that this is justified given that there is a dependent relationship forged between the service user and the practitioner and as we will go on to state, this also exists in relation to student and educator.

Being dependent on others is required for our survival, yet it can have a mixed response in health and social care settings with concerns expressed about service users becoming too dependent. This links to a worry that can be felt around dependency, which Evans (2021) proposes can be both unhealthy and hard to bear for workers. However, Evans also stresses that it can be a sign of health to have the capacity to be vulnerable and dependent on others, and we propose that this needs to be held in mind.

If a thoughtful, reflective space cannot be secured to think about the role of dependency and what it means for all involved, it can lead to a premature withdrawal of assistance and support. In this context, practitioners, educators and the services they represent are no longer experienced as dependable by those they provide services for and can be the antithesis of what is required.

To further the need for careful consideration of the dynamics inherent in dependency and dependability, Evans (2021) stresses that dependence and the resulting unequal power dynamic can lead to feelings of inferiority, shame and humiliation experienced by service users. The author goes on to say that if the worker lacks sensitivity to these experiences, this can fuel historical feelings of resentment and inequity in relation to authority figures. It is in the preparation of the social work master's students in the case example that we are attentive to this dynamic and aim to bring it into conscious awareness through education and support.

In doing this, we are trying to encourage attention to the ghosts from the nursery, to prevent their impact on experiences of dependency in the present and minimise the risk in those tasked to offer support against disengagement and avoidance. Such outcomes are contrary to what is needed to support a person's progression, whether it is in relation to practice settings or education, and it is this that we now turn our attention to.

The meeting of ghosts between service user and worker

It is perhaps reasonable to say that beyond the application of psychodynamic approaches as a therapeutic intervention in health and social care, the breadth of this approach is not routinely used to take account of the dynamics between the person using a service and practitioners. There may be many reasons for this, conscious and unconscious, including how the impact of interpersonal difficulties between the service user and practitioner may be managed when a viable alternative is not available. In the absence of such exploration, denial as a defence mechanism can be highly seductive. In this state of mind, interpersonal curiosity is likely to be quashed, leaving fertile ground for enactments between those involved.

Evans (2021) makes this point in relation to mental health settings, and we contend that this insight goes further to encompass all health and social care services which have a responsibility to attend to the needs of people and offer support. The author shares personal experience of being drawn through his countertransference into an enactment, an unconscious pull in the therapist to play out a prescribed role in response to the patient's transference. This emanates from the unconscious feelings and desires which derive from earlier relational experiences which were conveyed towards him as the therapist. This is why Evans stresses the importance of considering the damage that early life experiences can cause and how difficult relationships from the past with parents, carers and other figures of authority can be repeated in care settings. We understand this as ghosts from the nursery making their presence known in the here and now. However, psychodynamic perspectives derived from psychoanalytic thinking can help provide humane and considered care (Evans, 2021). This underpins the preparation of Social Workers as discussed in the case example.

The powerful impact of how the past intrudes into the present is detailed in 'Ghosts in the Nursery' where Annie, the young mother of baby Greg, does not consciously recall the terror of abandonment by her mother but allows those attentive to her unconscious communication to know by reenacting it in the transference relationship with them. This reenactment, the unconscious repeat of Annie's past experiences of abandonment in the present was said to have created the condition under which the therapist might be drawn into abandoning her (Fraiberg, Adelson & Shapiro, 1975).

Potential tragedy was averted, and a working relationship between Annie and the therapist was established. However, this part of the vignette from the paper prompts reflection on occasions where services are withdrawn or where abandonment results due to disengagement of the service user. Conceivably there are many reasons for services to be withdrawn, not least because of finite resources and difficulties managing these against huge demand. Dartington (2017) makes the point that human service organisations are defensive against the possibility of overwhelming need. Service withdrawal is one way in which caseloads and demand might be unconsciously managed.

Resourcing issues are not the only pressure that health and social care practitioners are subject to. Cooper and Lees (2015) argue that public scrutiny, inspections and political sensitivity alongside the marketisation of public services have also led to a new set of anxieties that bear down on social work and social care organisations in particular. Lefevre et al. (2024) highlight a range of defensive practices operating in organisations working in the field of extra-familial risks and harms. Lefevre et al. drew upon psychoanalytic understandings about social systems acting as a defence against anxiety, informed by Menzies-Lyth's (1988) work, to highlight the

> routinised practice, depersonalised ways of talking about young people and a preoccupation with information gathering and 'intelligence' all speak of organisational systems defending themselves against an untenable situation while needing to be seen to be doing something.
>
> (Lefevre et al., 2024, p. 109)

It is important to stress that the intention in raising this is to highlight the immense pressures that workers and organisations are under rather than suggesting there is a wholesale lack of commitment and creativity in helping people who access health and social care services. In much the same way as Fraiberg, Adelson, and Shapiro (1975) wondered about parents who endured difficult early experiences and managed not to repeat them with their own children but provided something better. Contrasted with those who cannot mobilise themselves in this way, we can consider what enables some workers to maintain their professional curiosity and sense of creativity and hope when working with "disengaged" service users.

To explore this issue further, we return to Fraiberg, Adelson, and Shapiro (1975). A key contention here is that ghosts in the nursery exist as 'visitors from the unremembered past of the parents' (p. 387) and intrude on early life, which in turn impacts in adulthood. It is in childhood that 'our early experiences form characteristic ways of relating to other people and of coping with the ebb and flow of emotions which are not only psychological predilections but also physiological patterns' (Gerhardt, 2015, p. 29). In this context, Sue Gerhardt draws on a wide theoretical underpinning, applying it in relatable ways and ultimately endeavouring to explore 'Why Love Matters'.

In relation to this chapter, we would say love matters because the ghosts in our nursery which inform early experiences directly relate to our personal and professional relationships in adulthood. Our early experiences of being cared for inform our ability to care for others and stick with them. Kraemer (2015) made this link with attachment theory, stressing that you give what you have received; to be attentive, one must have been attended to. It is, of course, not our intention to set this up as a simplistic cause-and-effect relationship. We cannot categorically say that those who had good enough early experiences will be creative and tenacious when faced with a "disengaged" service user/family. Nor can we set up a simple correlation between those who experienced difficulties in childhood and consequently have an inability to sufficiently attend to the needs of others; we know this is not always the case. That said, we cannot rule it out either; relationships are dynamic and predicated on the people involved, their circumstances and the situation they find themselves in.

As such, considering the dynamics between the service user and practitioner is crucial to the work of contemporary health and social care and can be said to require the worker being supported to be psychologically present. This has three essential conditions: 'not being preoccupied with one's own issues, being involved in meaningful task, feeling safe enough to employ the self without the fear of negative consequences' (Cardona, 2020, p. 66). However, meeting these conditions in contemporary practice is challenging, and there may be a tendency in the practitioner to split off part of the emotional experience to maintain their own mental health and therefore provide a reliable service (Cardona, 2020). This fits with Dartington's (2017) point that being without defence mechanisms is like going out in bad weather without suitable clothing. We need to protect ourselves, but this requires balance and the help of another to establish how to manage this before the tipping point.

Faced with the disturbance that can be provoked in staff and the pull to manage service users provocative or disturbing states of mind (Evans, 2021), denial and a lack of thoughtful attention to the dynamics between service user and worker can be catastrophic. Evans (2021) further states the importance of trying to understand disruptive and destructive elements in thinking; otherwise the underlying meaning of communication may be missed. This would contribute to the psychological task which enables us to stay 'open to the needs and experience of the people one is trying to help in the face of one's own motivations and reactions to illness and social disturbance' (Ballatt, Campling & Maloney, 2020, p. 55). Just as Annie in 'Ghosts in the Nursery' was helped to be curious about and bear the experiences of her baby, workers can be helped to engender and maintain a curiosity about the underlying meaning of the service user's communication alongside reflecting on their own communications.

Williams et al. (2022) facilitated and researched small group reflective practice for statutory child and families social work supervisors and their managers. A key aim in creating their reflective spaces was to enable participants to manage their professional vulnerabilities and to bear the anxiety of adopting positions of 'not knowing', against the backdrop of contemporary social work practice which privileges certainty and risk averse processes. They concluded that

> the central importance of containment in the face of anxiety ridden professional contexts the participants are working in is particularly apparent. As is the need for participants to be professionally vulnerable in order to maintain a position of professional curiosity.
>
> (Williams et al., 2022, p. 19)

The case example outlined at the start of this chapter is informed by this approach to guide its pedagogic and practice focus. The teaching and learning strategy aims to provide a psychodynamic facilitated space for students to critically reflect on their work and the impact of their practice organisations. The intention is to enable a thoughtful and contained environment where hypotheses can be explored rather than over-relying on perceived certainties, and professional curiosity can be encouraged.

Utilising Fraiberg, Adelson, and Shapiro's (1975) ghosts in this process offers a rich and engaging metaphor to help students to explore issues of past trauma in the lives of their service users and the potential for re-enactment in the dynamic between them. It also provides the opportunity to explore the ghosts students bring to work from their own nurseries considering their countertransference and the potential for enactment if not acknowledged and worked through. In this sense, students are facilitated to explore the interaction between the ghosts of their service users and their own ghosts in the hope that such knowledge facilitates a deeper understanding around dependency/dis/engagement responses and encourages the ability to sustain creative, humane and resilient practice in an increasingly pressurised practice environment.

The meeting of ghosts between educator and student

As educators, we have a psychological task in relation to our students, as we will go on to discuss in the following section; this is through an appreciation that professionals have a propensity to build up a defence against repeated pain, frustration, helplessness and intimacy as a way of surviving (Miller, 2017). Acknowledgement of this in an open way enables it to be thought and talked about, thereby reducing the likelihood of an unconscious pull to act it out. It is with recognition that psychological meaning develops within the context of the relationship with another person (Evans, 2021) that we stress this here.

Within an educational context, many aspects of psychological meaning develop and are enacted in the context of the educator–student relationship. However, we argue here that just as in the broader context of health and social care beyond services with a psychodynamic underpinning, routine, conscious account of the dynamics between students and educators is generally lacking. As Ballatt, Campling, and Maloney (2020, p. 37), point out, 'Too often, the attention of educators, managers and staff is directed to the technical, the performative elements of the clinical or caring task, rather than the relational'.

This lack of focus on the importance of student–educator dynamics is particularly notable in the context of health and social care, where educators have a key role in helping students reflect upon their helping relationships with their service users and other professionals. As such, we propose that exploring the impact of the educator–student relationship in this context may shed light on how other relationships are worked through.

As educators drawing upon psychodynamic frameworks to facilitate our work, it is helpful to acknowledge openly some of the emotional context of learning with our students. Osborne, Salzberger-Wittenberg, and Williams (1993) highlight some expectations and phantasies that students may have in relation to their educators: 'Thus contact with the teacher is likely to revive in the student many of the emotions that he experienced in the past in relation to his mother and father'.

Teachers can be perceived by students as needing to be the source of omnipotent knowledge and wisdom, provider and comforters, objects of admiration and envy, judges and authority figures, these possibilities emanating in part from the transference relationships – or the ghosts – from the students' previous formative experiences (Osborne, Salzberger-Wittenberg, and Williams, 1993). Acknowledging these potential transference relationships openly can help students to explore their reactions in an educational context and thereby reduce the likelihood of an unconscious pull to act them out. Students in health and social care settings often have additional educational relationships with mentors or practice educators/assessors in placement contexts as key players in their professional learning.

In our work with social work students described in the case example, we acknowledge some of the transference experiences that can be evoked for students in educational environments. One key phantasy we work with openly is to dispel our role as omnipotent educators. This is particularly important in the contemporary context of social work practice where certainty is privileged over not knowing as noted earlier. Students sometimes come to classes to be taught definitive answers and need time to adjust to a facilitated questioning space as opposed to an instructive didactic environment. As educators, we consciously adopt the role of facilitators and questioners who work alongside students to explore complex practice situations that are not amenable to quick fix solutions.

Working with students who are pursuing registration in one of the health and social care professions, along with academic qualifications in higher education, requires navigation of the rigours of the course and assistance in processing the experiences provoked during practice placements. This offers the opportunity to forge close working relationships between student and academics and such proximity brings contact between our ghosts from the nursery. As educators, it is argued that our capacity for attachment to work and organizational life is linked to our early experiences of emotional attachment and that without emotional attachment to a meaningful activity, work can feel insignificant, impacting satisfaction (Cardona, 2020). Given the emotional significance of our work, we propose the need for careful consideration of issues evoked as educators in working relationships with students.

Even the most highly trained professional can be susceptible to powerful projections (Elton, 2019), and this is not confined to the dynamic between service users and workers. Transference happens in all relationships, and as a response, so does countertransference. It therefore follows that our own early experiences will impact when we work closely with others; this is what we understand as a meeting of our ghosts. To illustrate this point, a vignette is included here with sufficient amendments to protect confidentiality.

Vignette

Ben was a 20-year-old male student who asked for a tutor visit whilst on placement. The member of staff supervising Ben observed injuries on his arms whilst his sleeves were rolled up, and on being asked about these, Ben disclosed he had been cutting himself.

Ben was an only child and lived with his parents. He had said that his father, who had a diagnosis of schizophrenia, had experienced mental health problems throughout Ben's childhood and adolescence. His mother he perceived as the distracted main carer for her husband and the breadwinner in the family; Ben's father was off work due to long-term sick leave, and he had been deemed unfit due to his mental health problems. What follows are reflections shortly after this disclosure on placement with added consideration evoked during the writing of this chapter.

The helping professions attract individuals who identify with those they are trying to help (Rustin, 2008). The choice of profession or client group can provide a medium through which to act out wounded, unresolved, possibly aggressive or sadistic elements of the personality (Ballatt, Campling & Maloney, 2020). Ben had hinted at his identification with his father through his interest and critique of the genetic theories of schizophrenia, and despite using humour to exclaim a wish not to end up like his father, this appeared to be a real worry for him. It was also significant that Ben had enabled the observation and then disclosure that he had been cutting himself whilst on placement with people in acute distress.

The psychic skin (Bick, 1968) is said to mediate the relationship between our inner and outer worlds, and where there is enough permeability and resilience, emotions can be externally communicated, and those of others accepted, without becoming overwhelmed. However, Heyno (2008) contends that those in unbearable distress may feel relief by projecting difficulties outwards, and if such feelings, are not heard, there is a risk of acting out. Acting out relieves intrapsychic tension through physical action as the internal drama passes from unconscious impulse to action, thereby bypassing conscious thought and feeling. This means the conflict is temporarily resolved through use of the body, often in a destructive or erotised way (Hale, 2008), both functions of which have been used to understand self-harm (Turp, 2003). One way to understand this situation with Ben, who said he had felt pushed aside during childhood, was to consider that physical injury may be an effective way to gain a caring response. This reflects Turp's (2003) contention that self-harm translates invisible to visible internal damage and acts as an unconscious form of communication.

Ben was referred to the University Occupational Health Department for review. The referral form was carefully written to instil that support was being sought for Ben alongside a desire to avoid withdrawal from the course. Consciously, this decision was determined by a belief that Ben's presentation and risk did not necessitate withdrawal, but Ben's situation was more complex than this initial understanding suggested. When the occupational health physician determined that Ben should be interrupted from the course for a period of 12 months, the referring tutor felt aggrieved.

The tutor's initial response centred on thoughts and feelings that Ben had done the right thing; he had been honest, and the result had been what he consciously said he did not want. Worries about a possible sense of his rejection and failure heightened concerns about Ben's wellbeing. Ben's need for care appeared to be firmly lodged within the tutor. There was also a sense of professional rivalry: how could the occupational health physician, with no training in mental health, make this decision?

The weight of feeling evoked in the tutor, however, was an indicator of something deeper; early experiences of care, parental vulnerabilities and omnipotence were being evoked and activated by the sense of responsibility for referring Ben to occupational health, and guilt associated with the concern that his mental health could deteriorate as a result. The opportunity to think this through, however, prevented an enactment and enabled a more thoughtful stance. The tutor was able to accept the decision and their part in it and offer Ben the supportive guidance he needed. It is conceivable that without the opportunity for thinking through and processing, the tutor may have resorted to their own acting out, distancing themselves from both the decision and Ben, perpetuating a feeling of rejection and avoidance of his need for attunement and support. It is in this context that a psychodynamic orientation proved so crucial in containing anxiety, enabling interrogation of thoughts, feeling and responses leading to a better understanding of the issues and a more thought out and considered response as a result.

Implications and recommendations

Connecting the past and present

Being supported to make links between the past and present is key to Fraiberg, Adelson, and Shapiro's (1975) contentions. We advocate the importance of this in terms of the dynamic between practitioner and service user in the context of health and social care and their preparation through professional programmes of study. The importance of this is presented by (Cardona, 2020), who states that the capacity to understand the link between current difficulties evoked by work and our early life experiences is transformative; it can moderate the effect of these influences and help us manage our roles in a more meaningful and effective way. We have illustrated our commitment to this through the inclusion of psychodynamic perspectives in the MA social work programme described in the case example that supports this chapter.

We also stress the importance of educators managing aspects of themselves which may negatively impact our working lives through the creation of opportunities belonging to the past that are felt compelled to repeat (Cardona, 2020). This is particularly important when we consider our ghosts from the nursery and the need to monitor ourselves in relation to those who access health and social care services. The need to be attentive to what gets stirred up in the practitioner and the vulnerability of service users to what Freud (1914) referred to as repetition compulsion is crucial to protect against enactments and re-enactments as discussed previously:

> Clinical discussion about nature of relationships between staff and patients, including enactments, can throw light on the clinical issues underlying the patient's presentation and ways of relating. This in turn can reduce the risk of thoughtless action in both patients and their carers.
>
> (Evans, 2021, p. 7)

This can only be achieved with support to be curious, and a psychodynamic approach offers one way to underpin this.

Engendering professional curiosity

> It is thus advisable in one's adult role to give some thought to how we came to be the way we are, and to use that insight to build on our strengths and assets, but also keep an eye on our vulnerabilities.
>
> (Obholzer, 2021, p. 11)

This requires what Britton (2004) describes as the third position which is the ability to be self-observing. If we can observe ourselves in interactions with others, we can be attuned to what gets stirred up and engage in thoughtful consideration of this rather than succumbing to its influence through unconscious processes.

This links to being attentive to countertransference and Abrahams and Rohleder (2021, p. 200–201) provide useful prompts to help attend to this. We use adapted aspects of it in our preparation of social work students for professional practice, which can be transferred to any professional practice context in health and social care as follows.

- What are you feeling as you listen and watch your "patient's" verbal and non-verbal behaviour?
- Do you feel under pressure to act in particular ways?
- Does any part of your response belong to you and not the "patient"?
- Is this a new feeling, thought or body sensation that you have when working with this "patient"?
- Have you thought or felt this way in previous sessions?

This is a useful guide for monitoring responses, reactions and feelings evoked when working in health and social care, particularly where the concept of countertransference is unfamiliar or training in being attentive to this has not been extensive.

Conclusion

This chapter, has drawn on 'Ghosts in the Nursery: A Psychoanalytic Approach to the Problems of Impaired Infant-Mother Relationships' (Fraiberg, Adelson & Shapiro, 1975) to illustrate the importance of being attentive to what we bring to our relationships with others. This is particularly important within the context of health and social care, where those using services and those preparing for qualification in one of the professions depend on a supportive, containing presence in support of progression. This applies in relation to meeting needs of service users as well as assimilating educative experiences and managing the impact of the work to provide high-quality health and social care. We have shown the importance of taking a psychodynamic approach and the benefits it has in educational settings and service provision for digesting the experiences that are inherently challenging. We have applied these ideas by drawing on a case example illustrating the preparation of social workers at one UK university and a vignette to support the application of these concepts.

References

Abrahams, D., & Rohleder, P. (2021) *A clinical guide to psychodynamic psychotherapy*. London & New York. Routledge Taylor & Francis Group.

Ballatt, J., Campling, P., & Maloney, C. (2020) *Intelligent kindness: Rehabilitating the welfare state*. 2nd ed. Cambridge University Press.

Bick, E. (1968) The experience of the skin in early object relations. *International Journal of Psychoanalysis*, 49, 484–486.

British Association Social Work. (2023) https://basw.co.uk/sites/default/files/resources/poverty_and_social_work_position_statement.pdf Accessed 30th April 2025.

Britton, R. (2004) *Sex, death, and the superego experiences in psychoanalysis*. London & New York. Karnac.

Cardona, F. (2020) *Work matters consulting to leader sand organizations in the Tavistock tradition*. London & New York. Routledge Taylor & Francis Group.

Cooper, A., & Lees, A. (2015) Spotlit: Defences against anxiety in contemporary human service organizations in Armstrong, D., & Rustin, M. (eds) *Social defences against anxiety exploration in a paradigm*. Tavistock Clinic Series. London. Karnac.

Dartington, T. (2017) The organisational context for good care in Vaspe, A. (ed.) *Psychoanalysis, the NHS, and mental health work today*. London. Karnac.

Eaton, A. D. (2025) Current issues with social work field education and ideas for change. *Social Work Education*, 1–10.

Elton, C. (2019) *Also human the Inner lives of doctors*. London. Windmill Books.

Evans, M. (2021) *Psychoanalytic thinking in mental health settings*. London & New York. Routledge Taylor & Francis Group.

Fenton, J. (2020) 'Four's a crowd'? Making sense of neoliberalism, ethical stress, moral courage and resilience. *Ethics and Social Welfare*, 14(1), 6–20.

Ferguson, H. (2018) How social workers reflect in action and when and why they don't: The possibilities and limits to reflective practice in social work. *Social Work Education*, 37(4), 415–427.

Fraiberg, S., Adelson, E., & Shapiro, V. (1975, Summer) Ghosts in the nursery. A psychoanalytic approach to the problems of impaired infant-mother relationships. *Journal of American Academy of Child Psychiatry*, 14(3), 387–421.

Freud, S. (1914) Remembering, repeating and working through (further recommendations on the technique of psycho-analysis II) in *The standard edition of the complete psychological works of Sigmund Freud*, Vol. 12, 145–156. Hogarth Press & The Institute of Psychoanalysis.

Gerhardt, S. (2015) *Why love matter: How affection shapes a baby's brain* (2nd edition). London & New York. Routledge Taylor & Francis Group.

Hale, R. (2008) Psychoanalysis and Suicide: Process and typology in Briggs, S., Lemma, A., & Crouch, W. (eds) *Relating to self-harm and suicide psychoanalytic perspectives on practice, theory and prevention*. London & New York. Routledge.

Heyno, A. (2008) On being affected without being infected: Managing suicidal thoughts in student counselling in Briggs, S., Lemma, A., & Crouch, W. (eds) Op cit.

Kraemer, S. (2015) Anxiety at the front line in Armstrong, D., & Rustin, M. (eds) *Social defences against anxiety exploration in a paradigm*. London. Tavistock Clinic Series. Karnac.

Lefevre, M., Huegler, N., Lloyd, J., Owens, R., Damman, J., Ruch, G., & Firmin, C. (2024) *Innovation in social care new approaches for young people affected by extra- familial risks and harms*. Bristol. Policy Press.

Menzies-Lyth, I. (1988) *Containing anxiety in institutions selected essays volume I*. London. Free Association Books.

Miller, M. (2017) Theory in use: Perspectives on containment in Vaspe, A. (ed.) Op cit.

Obholzer, A. (2021) *Workplace intelligence unconscious forces and how to manage them*. London & New York. Routledge Taylor & Francis group.

Osborne, E., Salzberger-Wittenberg, I., & Williams, G. (1993) *The emotional experience of learning and teaching*. London & New York. Routledge. Taylor & Francis Group.

Polnay, A., Pugh, R., Barker, V., Bell, D., Beveridge, A., Burley, A., Lumsden, A., Mizen, C.S., & Wilson, L. (2023) *Cambridge guide to psychodynamic psychotherapy.* Cambridge: Cambridge University Press.

The Psychodynamic Formulation Collective. (2022) *Psychodynamic formulation an expanded approach*. Oxford. Wiley Blackwell.

Rustin, M. (2008) Work discussion: Some historical and theoretical observations in Rustin, M., & Bradley, J. (eds) *Work discussion: Learning from reflective practice in work with children and families*. London. Karnac Books.

Schon, D. (1992) *The reflective practitioner: How professionals think in action*. London. Routledge.

Shdaimah, C., & Strier, R. (2020) Ethical conflicts in social work practice: Challenges and opportunities. *Ethics and Social Welfare*, 14(1), 1–5.

Turp, M. (2003) *Hidden self-harm narratives from psychotherapy*. London and Philadelphia. Jessica Kingsley Publishers.

Williams, J., Ruch, G., & Jennings, S. (2022) Creating the conditions for collective curiosity and containment: Insights from developing and delivering reflective groups with social work supervisors. *Journal of Social Work Practice*, 36(2), 195–207.

Conclusion

Shelly Allen

This book has been a collaboration in sharing psychodynamic approaches as an underpinning model for the delivery of high-quality health and social care. It is a model that is sustaining and nurturing through its focus on relational aspects of the work and one that we have benefited from ourselves.

The desire to bring classic psychoanalytic papers to the attention of those working in health and social care, who are not necessarily familiar with psychodynamic approaches, is clear throughout the book. It is in sharing these ideas that have been important to us that we hope to benefit a wider audience. As such, we have taken psychodynamic theory and applied it in a way that we are confident will be familiar to those who work in contemporary health and social care.

We have approached the chapters in the book through our use of psychodynamic approaches in teaching and through our clinical work. We have illustrated the wide-ranging utility of this approach, and how it can be applied across a range of settings and circumstances.

We have been attentive to the need to consider the past in relation to the present and have introduced a number of psychodynamic concepts, such as transference and countertransference; the reliance on defence mechanisms when under stress and the need for containing, holding relationships.

This is evidenced in the case examples we have included, which take a diverse and broad approach relating to individuals who use services and aspects of practice where the impact is felt by practitioners, leadership, teams, groups and an organisational context. We have stressed the need to appreciate intersectionality, to consider the unique and overlapping experiences we bring to the dynamic with those who work and use health and social care and vice versa. We think this will help in holding in mind similarities and differences in a shared way that takes account of the discrimination, prejudice and privilege which pervades our society. We have stressed the importance of being able to self-observe and monitor one's own responses and reactions. In applying psychodynamic concepts throughout this book, we have encouraged a healthy curiosity about oneself, others and the organizations in which the context of work takes place. We acknowledge that the more one is curious, the more one has to remain mindful of the complex dynamics to which they both are subject and contribute to. This requires support, and we have

DOI: 10.4324/9781003541660-12

considered this in a number of ways including reflective practice, work discussion, reading groups, the use of supervision and mentorship.

We have created a text which is accessible and written in an applied way to help those working in health and social care to make sense of the challenges that can be evoked by the nature and context of the work. In presenting the case examples linked to classic psychoanalytic papers, we hope to have engendered a sense of connection to one's own experiences and the points discussed. If there has been a sense of familiarity and interest, then we will have achieved our aim. As noted in the introduction, the challenge now is in progressing this to secure support in sustaining high-quality health and social care.

Index

www.ingramcontent.com/pod-product-compliance
Lightning Source LLC
Chambersburg PA
CBHW050611280326
41932CB00016B/3004